DEVELOPING DATA STRUCTURED DATABASES

Michael H. Brackett

Prentice-Hall, Inc. Englewood Cliffs, New Jersey 07632

Library of Congress Cataloging-Publication Data

Brackett, Michael H. (date)
  Developing data structured databases.

  Bibliography: p. 218
  Includes index.
  1. Data base management.   2. Data structures
(Computer science) I. Title. II. Title: Developing
data structured data bases.
QA76.9.D3B68 1987   005.74   86-8167
ISBN 0-13-204397-1

Editorial/production supervision and
  interior design: Lynda Griffiths
Cover design: Ben Santora
Manufacturing buyer: Gordon Osbourne

Printed in the United States of America

10 9 8 7 6 5 4 3 2 1

ISBN 0-13-204397-1   025

PRENTICE-HALL INTERNATIONAL (UK) LIMITED, *London*
PRENTICE-HALL OF AUSTRALIA PTY. LIMITED, *Sydney*
PRENTICE-HALL CANADA INC., *Toronto*
PRENTICE-HALL HISPANOAMERICANA, S.A., *Mexico*
PRENTICE-HALL OF INDIA PRIVATE LIMITED, *New Delhi*
PRENTICE-HALL OF JAPAN, INC., *Tokyo*
PRENTICE-HALL OF SOUTHEAST ASIA PTE. LTD., *Singapore*
EDITORA PRENTICE-HALL DO BRASIL. LTDA., *Rio de Janeiro*

To Marc, Sean, and Kevin

CONTENTS

3 DATA STRUCTURES 43

6 CASE STUDY   132

PREFACE

Today's business environment is characterized, among other things, by a high rate of change in the business world and a large backlog of information systems. Present indications are that these conditions will continue into the future. If a company is to survive in this type of business environment, it must learn to manage change effectively and to reduce the backlog of information systems.

One way to manage change effectively is to be capable of making good, responsive management decisions. These decisions, however, are based in part on the availability of good management information. A large portion of this information is tied up in the information system backlog and is not available.

The information system backlog is a result of many factors, not the least of which is high system maintenance and poor system design methods. Poor design methods lead to delayed implementation and additional maintenance, which, in turn, further increases the backlog and reduces the availability of information. The result is lower productivity and poor management decisions, causing a downward spiral for the company, resulting in failure.

To reverse this downward spiral, a company must be capable of making good management decisions and must have the management information available for those decisions. The information can be available only if the backlog is reduced and system development can be responsive to the company's needs in a changing business environment. The best long-term solution to reducing a large backlog is to implement a good system design method.

A good system design method must include both application design and information design. The application and the information have a strong interrelationship that cannot be broken. Both are equally important and neither can be eliminated without having a substantial impact on the other.

The data-structured system development method provides a way to design processes based on the data they manipulate. The processes are then packaged into applications according to the business activity they support. These business applications provide the information needed to manage the company.

The same method provides a way to define data requirements based on the data needed by each process. The data requirements are then used to design a database that contains subject data files. These subject data files support any business application requiring data for that subject.

This book describes the data-structured database design method. It presents a practical, real-world method for designing databases with minimal theory and numerous examples. The method produces logical subject databases that can be implemented in any physical operating environment. This method is used with, and is inseparable from, the data-structured system development method described by the author (see the Bibliography).

This book is applicable to both users and data-processing personnel. It is easy to understand and to follow the sequence of events for designing subject databases. It explains how to implement the method and how to use it to produce databases that are structurally stable, yet flexible enough to meet changing business needs.

This book does not describe acquisitions or use of specific database management systems or data dictionaries. It does not describe the physical implementation of a logical database into a physical operating environment. It does not explain the theory or mathematical derivation of logical database design.

The book begins with a brief history of data files and database evolution, followed by a description of basic design techniques. Next, the data-structured database design method is presented, followed by a complete case study. Finally, the trends in software, hardware, and the business environment are explained, followed by strategies for managing information in the future. Study questions are provided at the end of each chapter for review and to stimulate thought about database design.

The book contains numerous examples of design techniques for a wide variety of situations. Many of these examples were taken from actual applications. Some examples, however, have been modified for clarity or to illustrate a particular technique and do not represent the existing application.

Data-structured database design produces subject databases that are flexible enough to meet the needs of a dynamic business environment, yet are structurally stable. It allows the data to be managed by subject and the applications to be managed by business activity, while retaining the interrelationship between the data and the applications. It reduces backlogs, increases productivity, and provides the information necessary to make the management decisions that assure a company's survival.

ACKNOWLEDGMENTS

The author thanks Chris Bird, who provided the initial incentive to develop the data-structured database design method. It was his class on database design, and subsequent discussions about database design, that led to the development of this method.

Thanks go to the staff and users at Washington State University for their constructive criticisms and comments about the data-structured database design method. Their input into user requirements resulted in many of the features currently in the data-structured database design method.

Thanks are also extended to the staff and users at the Washington State Employment Security Department, whose comments resulted in substantial revisions to the design method. Particular thanks go to Jim Littlefield, whose diligent work with attribute names led to many of the naming rules. Particular thanks also go to Jon Daisey, whose knowledge of physical database implementation resulted in many of the outputs of logical design.

Finally, special thanks go to Dave Wells and Jeani Wells, who diligently tried each version of the design method and who participated in extensive discussions about database design. It was with their help and encouragement that development of the data-structured database design method was completed.

INFORMATION TRENDS

The business environment today is very dynamic and will become increasingly dynamic in the future. This dynamic environment is caused by the increasing rate of change and complexity of both technology and society. Any company that intends to survive in this environment must learn not only to live with change but to manage change.

Managing change includes proactive, dynamic management of all of a company's resources. Data is one of these resources that must be managed effectively for survival. Unsuccessful management of the data resource could well cause a company to fail even if other resources are managed effectively.

Data is managed like any other resource. It has a cost to acquire, a cost to maintain, a cost to protect, and in many cases a cost to destroy. It has a useful life and can be evaluated with a cost-benefit analysis. Good data management requires a strong management commitment to planning the effective and efficient use of the data resource to optimize a company's productivity.

SYSTEM CHANGES

Data-processing applications of the 1950s and 1960s were largely number-crunching, record-keeping applications. During the 1970s and early 1980s applications became more oriented toward information processing rather than data processing. These applications are still record-keeping applications, but they provide information for management rather than data that requires extensive interpretation.

Initially, there was too little data available to support good management decisions. With the information explosion there is plenty of data available, often too much, but it is not in the right form to support good decisions. Data must be condensed into the correct information to be useful for management decisions.

Historically, data-processing people have been relatively successful at gathering, storing, and displaying data. But they have been less successful at producing data for decisions. This lack of success has resulted from managers getting more data than they need, not understanding the data they do receive, and not getting the data they really do need.

Typically, managers thrive on personal, verbal, often informal data which they receive that is directly applicable to the decision at hand. Computer reports are typically large, abstract, tabular listings that provide few, if any, clues to problems or pending decisions. This disparity results in a reluctance to use computer reports.

Information systems that are useful to managers must be oriented to problem identification and decision support. They need to produce information that is understandable by users and relevant to the decisions at hand. They need to concentrate on people considerations rather than machine considerations.

Decision support systems provide the information necessary to support the decision-making process. They consist of integrated hardware and software systems that assist managers in the decision-making process by providing models, graphs, statistics, and simulations. Decision support systems do not replace a manager's judgment. They only provide information in a form that is useful and assists decision making. The decision is made by people after evaluating the information.

Decision support systems are good for semistructured decisions. If a decision process is highly structured and decision rules can be precisely defined, then a system can make the decision (i.e., a decision system). However, most decision processes are semistructured, that is, only partially quantifiable, and decision support systems can only provide information that assists or supports the decision process.

Therefore, decision support systems are useful when there are sufficient decision structures for mathematical and statistical models to be of value, but where a manager's judgment is essential. The manager poses a conceptual problem to the system. The system converts the problem to a mathematical model for solution, and returns information to the manager in terms of the original conceptual problem.

Decision support systems are not record-keeping applications. They are systems based on a collection of decision sets which provide the quantitative rules for making decisions. These decision data sets draw from data maintained by record-keeping applications.

Decision support systems are critical to a company's future. They can be used for planning, for developing "what if" models, for risk analysis, and for evaluating business performance. But they require close coordination between business management and information management.

A well-designed and maintained database is mandatory for a successful decision support system. These systems are most effective when they are integrated with a database that contains both basic record data and decision data sets. A well-designed database is the hub of decision support systems.

The database must be flexible and dynamic. Many of the decision data sets are transitory and the business data they use is constantly changing. Therefore, the database must contain current, accurate business data and must provide for rapid generation of decision data sets.

Knowledge-based systems can also assist users by providing a means to use, effectively and efficiently, a specialized body of knowledge such as genetics or medicine. They are not record-keeping or transaction-oriented systems. They provide a means to relate existing facts to solve a particular problem.

Knowledge-based systems are based on a scientific or technical body of knowledge. This knowledge base is not transitory as with record-keeping systems. It is relatively static, but growing as the body of knowledge about a discipline grows. A knowledge base is an unstructured set of facts, whereas traditional databases are structured facts that are explicitly stated. It is a large collection of facts about a specific topic. It is really a library of technical knowledge.

A knowledge-based system is the reference librarian that accesses and analyzes these facts. It is a rule-based system where a selection predicate is used against the knowledge base to provide all facts for which the predicate is true. Native languages are used for queries to develop the rules and for clarification of ambiguous rules.

The databases to support knowledge-based systems must be able to maintain unstructured sets of facts, and sets of rules to relate those facts. Like decision support systems, knowledge-based systems must be integrated with the knowledge base. Unlike decision support systems, they contain unstructured sets of facts.

Expert systems perform specialized, professional tasks at a level equivalent to that of human experts. They contain extensive decision rules used by experts for diagnosis, discovery, and explanation. They provide a problem-solving capability that relies on both databases and knowledge bases.

Expert systems have the ability to reason and to draw inferences from statements of fact. They are sometimes referred to as inference engines or inference machines. They provide solutions to complex, unstructured problems and help users navigate available knowledge bases and to draw conclusions and inferences from that knowledge. Users are not a homogeneous group and their individual information needs differ. Expert systems assist users in differentiating and defining their information needs.

The user interacts with the expert system to formulate a question. When the question has been formulated correctly and completely, it is structured as a formal query. That query is used to determine a solution which is returned to the user.

Expert systems require extensive databases and knowledge bases. Both must be well planned, designed, and developed. Ideally, they should both be integrated with the expert system.

Graphics systems can be used to enhance traditional systems, decision support systems, and knowledge-based systems. They can also be used independently to display graphic representations of data. Their strength lies in their ability to reduce a maze of numbers to a quick look at important information for managers.

Graphics management systems are peers to database management systems. They are designed to store and retrieve graphics data much the same as database management systems are designed to store and retrieve record-keeping data. They can produce traditional line, bar, pie, and scatter plots, as well as diagrams such as organization charts, flowcharts, and floor plans.

The evolution from traditional record-keeping systems to decision support systems, knowledge-based systems, expert systems, and graphics systems requires a parallel evolution to better databases. Larger, more sophisticated application systems will rely on more sophisticated databases. In fact, those systems will be only as good as the databases on which they depend.

LANGUAGE CHANGES

First-generation languages utilized machine-level operation codes and actual machine storage locations to define processing. Second-generation languages utilized assemblers to replace machine-level operation codes and machine storage locations. Programmers wrote instructions that resulted, via assemblers, in machine operation codes and actual storage locations.

Third-generation languages are the conventional source languages in use today. A more generic source language is written which, via a compiler, results in machine operation codes and storage locations. Their main use is for record keeping, transaction-oriented tasks using structured data bases.

The use of third-generation languages has remained largely with data-processing professionals. Users have been allowed and encouraged to define their requirements and participate in design. However, the development and enhancement of third-generation systems has been tightly controlled by professional data-processing staffs.

The use of third-generation languages, particularly with application-owned files, has resulted in a lack of understanding about the structures and use of subject data files. Access to subject data files can be more detailed than traditional file programming, but has longer-term benefits. This lack of understanding and more detailed access, plus a lack of good subject database design, has resulted in less-than-successful systems.

This situation of professional control and poor subject databases has occurred at a time when users want more and better data to perform their duties. At the same time, more hardware and software are available to users. This has resulted in users developing their own applications on their own hardware.

Fourth-generation languages are nonprocedural languages. They let the computer decide how tasks should be performed. They can be interactive and menu driven and can provide ad hoc, prompted processing, which is just what users need to develop their own systems.

The operating system and database for fourth-generation languages are usually transparent to the user. A good data dictionary must be used to support fourth-generation languages and databases. However, due to a lack of well-defined organizational responsibilities and standards, data dictionaries are usually not maintained.

Fourth-generation languages lend themselves to prototyping. As data is obtained from a database, a request can be modified based on refined requirements. This, in turn, provides better data, which provides a further refinement of requirements.

Results may be obtained more quickly from fourth-generation applications. However, they may cost more. The cost-effectiveness of a quicker, more expensive answer, compared to a longer wait for a less expensive answer, must be weighed by each individual company.

To be successful, fourth-generation applications must have well-designed databases and an accurate, up-to-date data dictionary. Poorly designed databases and an incomplete data dictionary will only result in unsuccessful systems.

Fifth-generation languages are largely undefined, but generally deal with knowledge manipulation. There is a people/machine interaction to organize specifications and create an application that performs a specific task. In short, a system is used to query a user and build an application to meet the user's specific needs.

The specification interaction allows the user to communicate with a knowledge base in terms of data structures and logical requirements. Specifications are reviewed for consistency and completeness, and processes are developed to produce an answer. In true prototype fashion, the answer is used to refine the specifications to obtain a better answer.

Obviously, there is a connection between the trend from business systems to decision support systems, knowledge-based systems, and expert systems and the trend from third- to fifth-generation languages. Business record-keeping systems are using third-generation languages and some less procedural fourth-generation languages in connection with structured databases. Decision support systems will use some third- and full nonprocedural fourth-generation languages with structured databases.

Knowledge-based systems will use fourth-, and possible fifth-, generation languages and less structured knowledge bases. Expert systems will use fifth-generation languages for complex, unstructured problem-solving systems. There will be a definite trend away from record-keeping systems to non-record-keeping, semistructured, and unstructured problem-solving systems, and a trend from third- to fifth-generation languages.

DATABASE CHANGES

The structure of databases has evolved together with the evolution of systems and source languages. Traditional record-keeping systems used traditional sequential, indexed, or direct files where any relation between files was defined by the application programmer. The emergence of database management systems led to several concepts of database architecture.

Database architecture refers to how data is linked in the database and how it appears to the user outside the database. The application programmer has very little, if any, control over the architecture of a database management system.

Hierarchical database architecture is based on a tree structure in which any record is subordinate to only one other record. The data structures are fixed in a one-to-many relationship between data entities and the only entry is at the top of the tree. Each user view is predefined, resulting in large amounts of structural detail.

The conceptual structure matches the physical structure, which is very appealing initially. However, the data is not totally free of the application. Any change in the applications data requirements means a change in the predefined data structures, which results in a high level of maintenance.

Network database architecture is based on a ring or plex structure in which any record can be subordinate to several other records. The structures are still predetermined, but there is less structural detail than with hierarchical databases, and entry can be made anywhere in the network. However, the application programmer still needs to know the physical data structure to navigate through the database.

Relational database architecture has no predefined subordinates. The relations between records is implicit based on common data items. The physical relationships are defined at execution time based on the applications needs.

Since there are no predefined relationships, the structural detail is minimal and maintenance is low. Low maintenance makes it easier to control database changes. Easier control allows better management of the data.

Since logical views are independent of physical storage, the data is readily available for many user types. The sharing of readily available data helps users meet their information needs. Relational databases are good for prototype applications. They are also good for semistructured and unstructured decision making and problem solving. Development of new applications or enhancements of existing applications may require changes in data from the database, but these changes are easily provided.

Relational databases are relatively easy to design, maintain, and use. They enforce data independence and encourage data sharing. They readily support application development, prototyping, and distributed data applications. Relational architecture will probably support most systems in the near future.

An enhancement of relational databases is the time-relational database, which incorporates comprehensive time-processing capabilities into the relational database. It establishes the concept of time independence, where the time the data is entered into the database is independent of the time period to which the data pertains.

In traditional database management systems data is effective when it is entered and ceases to be effective when it is removed. No distinction is made between when data is entered and what time period it represents. There is no real history of changes and altered values.

The objective of the time-relational database is to provide database views at different points in time. These views include the data values, the data structure, and the rules and logic that manipulated the data. These views may be in the past, present, or future.

The time-relational database has the ability to access the time dimension of data. It provides the capability for retroactive updates where the effectiveness of the data takes place in the past. It also has the capability for proactive updates where the effectiveness of the data takes place in the future.

The time-relational database maintains a history of altered data values and changes in the structure of the database. It also maintains a history of the program logic and data manipulation rule changes. Finally, it maintains a history of the person or group responsible for the changes.

The location of databases is evolving from central files to distributed files. The distributed files may be on a personal computer in the next room or on a mainframe in another country. The distance and size of the distributed files are not important, but their design and structure is important.

As trends to distributed data increase, the design of distributed databases must include the capability to designate where the data is stored. It must also indicate whether the same data is located in multiple databases for local access or in only one database for remote access. This design feature supports the trend toward data sharing.

DATA MANAGEMENT CHANGES

Data was relatively easy to manage in the early days of data processing. Applications were tied directly to sequential card or tape files so that the application and its data were virtually inseparable. There were only a few data files per application, and applications did not share data files.

Most applications were core business processes such as fiscal and personnel management, with a relatively finite and distinct set of data. Each application had a user who owned and controlled both the application and the data. However, the user knew very little about how to develop and maintain applications.

Data-processing personnel were the technical wizards who made everything work. Processing was highly centralized in a batch environment where security and integrity were implied. There were no communication networks, and access to the data was limited to the user and the system analyst.

As data processing became more popular and cost-effective, applications began to spread throughout the company. Other business activities, technical activities, and even management support activities became automated. However, each new application was still tied directly to its data file and the user still owned the data.

These new applications were more complex due to the processes they performed. Also, the data used by each application were not as finite and distinct as earlier applications. More data were used and portions of the data were common between several applications.

The proliferation of these new applications with fixed data files and common data items caused data to be captured and stored redundantly. The same data items were collected independently and stored on separate data files. A user was not allowed to access another user's data file for either inquiry or update.

The increasing data redundancy created updating problems. An update to a common data item was usually not made to all occurrences of that data item among the various files. This caused data to be out of sync with reality and created multiple versions of the truth.

The more complex applications began to access more data files. File access and relations between files were hard coded in each application program. This made programs even larger and more complex and increased program maintenance.

The impact of incomplete data updating and increased program maintenance was decreased productivity. Data-processing personnel spent an increasing amount of time determining what data was current and correct.

Applications began sharing data to offset this decreased productivity. However, this data sharing was done by extracting, sorting, and merging data to provide the right set of data for an application. This new set of data was usually stored in a new data file unique to the new application.

Although data sharing provided unique data views for each application, it actually increased the redundancy and maintenance problems because new files were created and file accesses were still hard coded in the program. What was intended to improve productivity really decreased productivity. The one good concept of data sharing was the usefulness of different views of the same data for different applications.

As data sharing became popular, the question of authority to update began to be asked. As multiple users accessed the same data it was not always clear who had the authority to change that data. This question led to the ownership controversy that is prominent in many companies today.

The ownership controversy was usually resolved by allowing each user to update his or her own view of the data which was still on his or her own data file. Notification of changes was sent to all users of that data, for updating. The ownership controversy was partially resolved by manual distribution of updates to users rather than the creation of common data files.

DATABASE ENVIRONMENT

The database environment concept emerged to resolve update problems, high program maintenance, and the ownership controversy. It replaced the extract–sort–merge approach to providing different views of the same data, and it managed relations between data files. The result was reduced program complexity and maintenance, and more accurate data.

The data was free of application constraints and programs were free of file accesses and record formats. The database environment separated the structure of applications from the structure of subject data. This data independence provided complete integration of the application and its data, yet isolated the application from any structural change to the data. The subject data files could be modified to meet the needs of one application without affecting other applications.

Data independence minimized both data redundancy and data update problems. It also provided maximum flexibility to meet the needs of a changing business environment. This increased productivity for both the user and the data processing personnel and placed the company in a better position to manage change effectively.

The database environment led to a new concept of corporate ownership of the data. The company, not the individual users, owned and managed the data. The data was available on demand to any authorized application, and changes to the data could be made more quickly. However, the data was subject to strict accounting and auditing controls and the users still defined their data needs.

A data administration unit was usually established to manage the data resource. In the strict sense that unit owns the data, but they must meet user application needs. They must also assure the security and confidentiality of the data.

As the database environment gained popularity, other major changes were in progress. Communications networks were proliferating and distributed processing was a reality. User-friendly systems and hardware flourished and users began acquiring their own hardware, writing their own programs, and maintaining their own data files.

The trend in the future is more and larger communication networks, more distributed processing, and more direct user involvement. Applications will spread to all segments of the business environment. Office automation, personal computers, information centers, and color graphics will become commonplace.

These trends will create a fragmented information-processing environment if they are not managed. They are changes to the business environment that must be managed like any other change. The companies that manage these changes effectively are the companies that will survive and thrive. Those that do not will fail.

A major part of managing the changing business environment is managing the database. A well-planned and implemented database will provide the management control to prevent fragmentation. It will provide the flexibility to adjust quickly to the needs of a changing business environment. It will reduce program maintenance and minimize redundant data updating. It will increase productivity throughout a company and give it the best chance for survival in a very competitive world.

STUDY QUESTIONS

1. Why is the business environment so dynamic?
2. What major trends are in progress today?
3. What are decision support systems?
4. What are expert systems?
5. How do knowledge-based systems differ from decision support and expert systems?
6. What are the differences between hierarchical, network, and relational database architectures?
7. What are the advantages of relational databases?
8. Why was early data management relatively easy?
9. What problems were created as applications became more complex and began sharing data?
10. What are the advantages of a database environment?
11. How will the database environment change with changing information trends?
12. What will happen if the trends in information processing are not managed effectively?

2

BASIC TECHNIQUES

The design of data-structured information systems is based on the structure of the data they process. The data flowing through the system is analyzed, defined, and structured according to specific criteria. The structure of the process logic and the databases are determined from these data structures.

The method of developing data-structured information systems has evolved over a period of several years. Various techniques were tried and accepted, modified, or rejected. The result was a method for developing application logic and subject databases from a common base.

During development of the data-structured method a variety of techniques were defined that are basic to the method itself. These basic techniques are the principles and procedures used to design and develop data-structured information systems. An understanding of these techniques is mandatory before the method can be presented.

Data flowcharts are used to display the architecture of an entire information system. This architecture shows the processes, the data used by each process, and how the data is stored. When completed, the data flowcharts are the blueprints for developing the system.

As the data flowcharts are being developed, the data is defined. Data definition includes structuring the data, based on the needs of each process, and correctly naming the data. It also includes defining the relationships between sets of data, and establishing keys to access each set of data and to identify uniquely each occurrence in a data set.

These basic techniques can be used in a wide variety of situations. Although each situation may be slightly different, the basic techniques still apply.

The real skill is not in learning the techniques themselves, but in applying the techniques to the situation at hand.

When these techniques are learned and a skill is developed for applying the techniques to system development, good application logic and good databases can be developed. Good application logic and good databases lead to good information systems. Good information systems lead to improved productivity and an increased chance for company survival.

DATA STRUCTURE CONCEPT

Data-structured systems are based on the structure of the data flowing in an information system. The structure of the data sets the structure of the process logic and defines subject databases. The data structure must be defined before the process logic or databases can be defined and that definition must precede any physical construction.

Traditional Approach

Traditional design methods are based on processing a physical record and a physical file of those records. Processing is defined for a physical flow of data; that is, a record is read, stored, sorted, edited, merged, extracted, written, and so on. The orientation is a physical record, a physical file, and physical processing.

A major disadvantage with a physically oriented design is that it leads to physical constraints, particularly computer hardware and source language constraints. When these constraints occur early in the design process, they severely limit the designer's ability to design an effective, efficient system for the users. The designers are too preoccupied with physical constraints to be able to design a good system objectively.

A second disadvantage with a physical orientation is that the scope of the design is limited to the automated portion of the system. This limitation results from a concern about processing physical records and their related physical constraints. When a design is limited to the automated portion of the system, the nonautomated portion is often totally neglected, to the detriment of the system.

A third disadvantage with a physical orientation is limited user involvement. This occurs because computer jargon, which users may not understand, is used, or because only the automated portion of the system is designed. Although users may be concerned about the automated portion of the system, they are less knowledgeable about, and less involved in, the design.

Physical constraints, physical orientation, limited scope of design, and limited user involvement have a negative impact on the effectiveness and efficiency of the system. To make major advances in designing information systems, a physically oriented design must be avoided.

Data Structure Approach

In data-structured system development the data is defined and structured first, avoiding hardware and software limitations. Since the physical limitations are avoided and data definition affects users directly, there is greater user involvement. This user involvement is enhanced by limiting the computer jargon, a task that is surprisingly easy when designing the total system without physical constraints.

Defining and structuring the data itself does not complete the design process. The process logic must also be defined in terms of situations and actions. The situations that can occur in a system are defined and the actions to be taken in each situation are specified. These actions result in data manipulation to meet user needs.

The subject databases for data storage are also defined from the data structures. The data structures are decomposed and attributes are logically added by subject to form subject databases. These subject databases store data for the process logic to manipulate.

After the process logic and subject databases are defined, the physical system is constructed and implemented into a specific production environment. If that production environment changes, the physical processing is modified based on the existing logical design. If the data or process logic change, the logical design is modified and appropriate changes are made to the physical system.

Data definition begins by identifying all the processes, data storages, and data flows to and from those processes and storages. This is done with data flowcharts that are structured in a parent–child relationship from a system overview to a detail level. Data structures are prepared for each unique data flow.

The format for displaying data structures is a structure chart consisting of a hierarchy of detail from the highest level on the left to the lowest level on the right. Each level of detail contains one or more sets of data placed vertically within the level. Each set is indicated by a bracket, with a set label centered vertically to the left of the bracket. The contents of the set appear to the right of the bracket.

The contents of a set are the attributes belonging to that set and any subsets of data. Each subset of data contains attributes and any additional subsets of data. Considering all levels and sets provides a hierarchy composed logically of sets and subsets of data.

Figure 2.1 shows a data structure for fishing season data. The highest level of detail is Fishing Season. During the fishing season there are many Fishing Vessels engaged in fishing. Each vessel makes Fishing Trips, and dur-

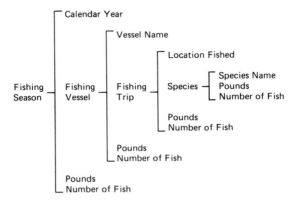

Figure 2.1   Fishing season data structure.

ing each trip catches different Species of fish. Fishing season, fishing vessel, fishing trip, and species are sets of data.

Fishing Season is identified by an attribute for Calendar Year. Fishing Vessel is identified by the Vessel Name. Fishing Trip is identified by the Location Fished, and Species is identified by the Species Name. Each of these four data sets contains attributes for Pounds and Number of Fish.

This data structure is composed of five levels, from Fishing Season on the left to Species Name, Pounds, and Number of Fish on the right. There are, however, only four sets of data. The Fishing Season set contains Calendar Year, Pounds, and Number of Fish. Fishing Vessel, a subset of Fishing Season, contains Vessel Name, Pounds, and Number of Fish. Fishing Trip, a subset of Fishing Vessel, contains Location Fished, Pounds, and Number of Fish. Species, a subset of Fishing Trip, contains Species Name, Pounds, and Number of Fish.

Data structures are the basis of data-structured system development. They are used to define the data in a system, the process logic to manipulate the data, and the databases to store the data. Data structures, process logic, and subject databases are defined without any physical constraints and the physical system is constructed only after the design is completed. Once this concept is thoroughly understood, data processors and users can work together to develop successful information systems.

Data Terms

When defining data structures, the terms "entity," "attribute," and "value" are used. An *entity* is any person, place, thing, or event: in grammatical terms an entity is a noun. Examples of entities are people, cars, boats, cities, accounts, positions, etc. Entities are either tangible, e.g., people, cars, boats, or nontangible, e.g., events, accounts, positions.

Attributes are characteristics that describe or characterize an entity: in grammatical terms an attribute is an adjective. Attributes are the actual data elements being processed, and each entity will have one or more attributes. Examples of attributes are height, color, weight, size, name, quantity, etc.

Values are the specific data in an attribute describing an entity. Values may be actual measurements, e.g., 6 foot 3 inches, 12.3 tons; descriptive information, e.g., blue, Sammy Jones; or codes, e.g., A246.

Entities are the subjects for developing subject databases. Attributes are the data elements stored in those subject databases. When data is structured it is the entities and attributes that are structured. The values are not shown since they are the contents of an attribute. Codes may be structured, however, as described later.

The major entity becomes the highest set in a data structure. Minor entities become subsets and are nested in successively lower levels. These entities and subentities form the basic data structure.

In Figure 2.1, Fishing Season is the major entity. Within any Fishing Season one or more Fishing Vessels are active, making Fishing Vessel a subentity of Fishing Season. Each Fishing Vessel makes one or more Fishing Trips during the season, making Fishing Trip a subentity of Fishing Vessel. Finally, one or more Species of fish are landed on each Fishing Trip, making Species the lowest subentity in the data structure.

At this point the basic data structure is established. Only the attributes need to be added to complete the structure. Any attribute identifying the entity is usually placed at the top of the set for that entity. For instance, Calendar Year is used to identify Fishing Season; Vessel Name is used to identify Fishing Vessel; Location Fished is used to identify Fishing Trip; and Species Name is used to identify Species. Although only one identifying attribute is shown for each entity, multiple identifying attributes may be placed at the top of the set.

Any attribute that is calculated, accumulated, derived, or generated is usually placed at the bottom of the set for that entity. In Figure 2.1, Pounds and Number of Fish are shown for each of the four entities.

The identifying attributes in Figure 2.1 have uniquely qualified names; however, the calculated attributes do not. To provide fully qualified names, the entity name is prefixed to the attribute name. For instance, the Pounds and Number of Fish for the Fishing Season entity become Fishing Season Pounds and Fishing Season Number of Fish.

Data Structure Uses

Data structures can be used in many ways to show how the data is being used, stored, or processed. For instance, alternatives can be placed in a data structure to explain the data further. Figure 2.2 shows the same fishing season data as above, but with different data collected depending on the year. Up

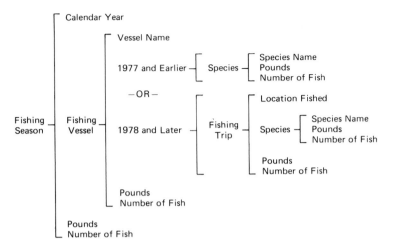

Figure 2.2   Fishing season data structure with alternative structure.

through 1977, Species data was collected by Fishing Vessel. Beginning in 1978, Species data was collected for each Fishing Trip.

Data structures can also be used to show the sequence and organization of data. Figure 2.3 shows one logical record for each Species, with the attributes Calendar Year, Vessel Name, Location Fished, Species Name, Pounds, and Number of Fish. The logical records are in the sequence Fishing Season/ Fishing Vessel/Fishing Trip/Species.

If the data is in the same sequence, but there is a separate logical record for each fishing vessel, for each fishing trip that each vessel makes, and for each species landed during each trip, the data structure would be drawn as shown in Figure 2.4. The attributes appear in the set they characterize. Additional attributes have been added to Fishing Vessel and Fishing Trip to illustrate multiple identifying attributes. If the same data is in a single logical record with no sequence to the logical records, the data structure is drawn as shown in Figure 2.5.

The data structures presented in Figures 2.1 through 2.5 are simple examples, but they cover the range of uses for data structures. When designers and users become familiar with the concept and use of data structures, they

Figure 2.3   Fishing season data structure for logical records.

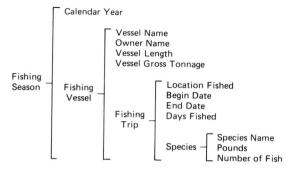

Figure 2.4 Fishing season data structure representing three logical records in sequence.

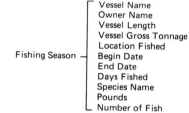

Figure 2.5 Fishing season data structure for individual logical records with no sequence.

will be able to define data and process logic with a skill that was unknown in traditional system design.

DATA FLOWS

Data flowcharts are used to identify all the data flows, data storages, and processes in a system. Similar to the traditional system flowchart, data flowcharts identify all the components of a system. Unlike the traditional system flowchart, they do not show responsibility, control, iterations, or internal formats. They show only data flow, data storages, and logic processes.

Data Flow

A data flow represents a unique set of data flowing in a system. Each unique data flow is different from every other data flow in the system, and the data flow name indicates this unique difference. Each unique data flow has its own data structure.

A data flow is shown by a line with an arrow on one end indicating the direction of the data flow, as shown in Figure 2.6. The name of the data flow is written on the line.

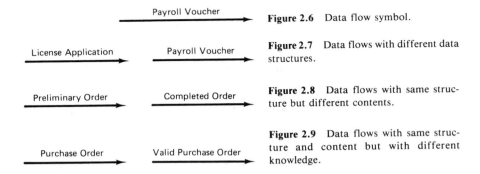

Figure 2.6 Data flow symbol.

Figure 2.7 Data flows with different data structures.

Figure 2.8 Data flows with same structure but different contents.

Figure 2.9 Data flows with same structure and content but with different knowledge.

Data flows can be different in any of three ways. First, they may have different structures. Second, they may have the same structure, but a different content. Third, they may have the same structure and content, but the knowledge about the data flow is different.

The two data flows in Figure 2.7 have entirely different data structures. Their unique names indicate this difference.

The two data flows in Figure 2.8 have the same data structure, but the contents are different. An intermediate process adds information that changes the contents. The data flow names indicate the change from preliminary to completed order.

The two data flows in Figure 2.9 have the same data structure with the same contents, but the knowledge about the data is different. The data has been reviewed in an intermediate process and found to be valid, so the knowledge about the data has changed. The names reflect the change in knowledge about a purchase order.

Data Storage

Data storages are places where data is held for future use. These storages may be filing cabinets, computer files, card indexes, etc. The physical repository is of no consequence. It is the logical process of data storage that is being defined.

An example of a data storage is shown in Figure 2.10 as a "box with bulging sides." The name of the subject data in the storage is shown inside the data storage symbol. The arrows show the flow of data into and out of the data storage.

The data flows into and out of a data storage do not normally have a data flow name. The data flow name is the same as the data storage name. Since a data flow cannot change itself and there is no process involved in the data storage, the data flows into and out of a data storage have the same name as the data in the storage.

Each data storage contains only one data subject, that is, one entity.

Figure 2.10 Data storage symbol.

During the construct phase of system development, multiple logical data storages may be combined into one physical data file or one logical data storage may be split into several physical data files. But during the design phase a separate data storage is defined for each data entity.

Logic Process

A logic process indicates that some action is taken on the data. The data flowing into the process is modified or converted to the data flowing out of the process. Each process will have at least one data input and at least one data output.

Figure 2.11 shows processes indicated by rectangles, for editing and correcting boat data. The input to the Boat Edit process is an Unedited Boat, and the output is either an Error Boat or a Good Boat. A Good Boat goes into a Boat storage. An Error Boat goes to a Boat Correction process. A Corrected Boat goes back to the Boat Edit process.

Naming Flows, Processes, and Storages

Within any system, and preferably within a company, no two unique data flows may have the same name. If two or more different data flows do have the same name, either the process did nothing to the data or there are identical data flows. This situation must be reviewed and corrected.

The same unique data flow may appear more than once on a data flowchart. If the data flow, for instance a document, moves through several processes unaltered, it retains the same data flow name. If it is altered, then it must have another name.

All data flowing in a system must be accounted for; i.e., data cannot be

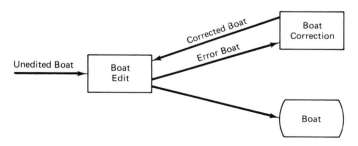

Figure 2.11 Data flow chart for editing boat data.

arbitrarily created or destroyed. Accounting for all data may result in the same data flow in two or more places. For instance, a report may flow out of one process into another process for use, then out of that process to archival storage. These two data flows would have the same name.

Within any system, and preferably within a company, no two data processes may have the same name. If there are two or more processes with the same name, either there is redundant processing or misnamed processes. Either situation must be reviewed and corrected.

Process names usually begin with a verb or contain a verb to indicate action. Those verbs must be meaningful to anyone using data flowcharts. The use of source language verbs should be avoided.

Data storage names are the name of the subject entity contained in the storage. Within the company no two different data storages may have the same name. If two storages have the same name but contain different data, one of those storages must be renamed.

Data flow names describe the data that is flowing in the system. Process names describe the change in data between input to the process and output from the process. Data storage names describe the subject data being stored. The data flows and data storages are usually named first, with the processes named after the data flows and storages.

Data Flow Examples

To clarify further the use of data flowcharts, good and bad examples will be shown and explained. In Figure 2.12 several processes are connected by data flows. Two of the data flows are final outputs (Data Flows 3 and 6) and one of the data flows is an initial input (Data Flow 1). These data flows are termed *net data flows*. The other data flows (Data Flows 2, 4, and 5) are *internal data flows*.

Figure 2.13 shows both the convergence of data flows and the divergence of data flows without any process at the intersection. Data cannot be combined or separated without a process, no matter how simple that process.

The errors in Figure 2.13 should be resolved by inserting a process at the

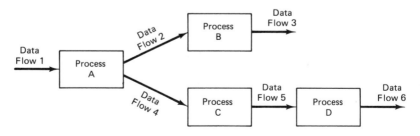

Figure 2.12   Typical data flowchart showing internal and net data flows.

Figure 2.13   Data flowchart showing incorrect convergent and divergent data flows.

point of convergence or divergence, or by using two separate data flows between processes. Figure 2.14 shows correct use of data flows.

More than one data flow may occur in the same direction between two processes if they are different and unrelated data flows. In Figure 2.15 there are two data flows between the Purchasing process and the Accounts Payable process. Purchase Orders and Printing Requisitions are two separate and unrelated data flows.

A process that has only inputs or only outputs, as shown in Figure 2.16, is probably in error. A process must have at least one input and one output to be functional. When processes are defined with only inputs or only outputs, the process should be carefully reviewed to determine what it really does.

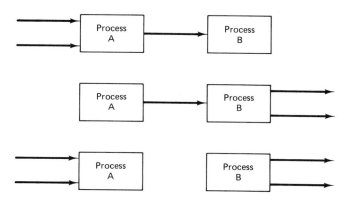

Figure 2.14   Data flowchart showing correct convergent and divergent data flows.

Figure 2.15   Data flowchart showing multiple data flows between processes.

Figure 2.16   Data flowchart showing processes with only inputs or only outputs.

The same situation is true for data storage. A data storage that has only inputs or only outputs usually has no reason for existence. If this situation occurs, the processing should be carefully reviewed and redefined to eliminate the problem.

Data storages may have multiple inputs and outputs as shown in Figure 2.17. Multiple outputs are more common than multiple inputs, but either are acceptable situations for data storages.

Utility processes that are used more than one place in a system are defined in detail only once. The high-level (single-process) data flowchart of that utility process is shown on each data flowchart where that utility process is used. This procedure avoids redundant detail definition of a utility process.

Occasionally, high-level data flowcharts have too many inputs or outputs to show on separate data flows. On these flowcharts it is acceptable to show a single data flow with a generic group name and then list the individual data flows in a convenient place on that data flowchart.

An example of a system with multiple outputs is shown in Figure 2.18. A data flow for each output would make the data flowchart too confusing to understand. The generic groups of data flows for Management Reports and Statistical Reports are shown flowing out of the process. The individual reports in each generic group are listed to the right.

When a database management system is available for a system, a convention is used to simplify the data flowchart. To show how data is obtained from a database management system, a process should be inserted between the storage and the application process to show selection of the specific set of data required from the database. This results in many unnecessary processes on a data flowchart.

To resolve this situation the database management system process is omitted from the data flowchart and the name of the set of data obtained from the database is placed on the data flow. Figure 2.19 shows how these logical data views are obtained from data storages in a database environment.

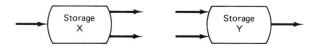

Figure 2.17 Data flowcharts showing storages with multiple inputs and outputs.

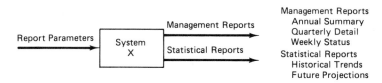

Figure 2.18 Method to show numerous data flows on a high-level data flowchart.

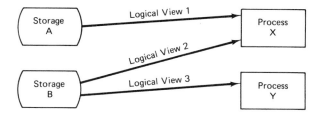

Figure 2.19 Logical view of data from storages in a database environment.

Structuring Data Flow

It may be unreasonable to show all the data flows, storages, and processes on one data flowchart. The amount of detail and size of the chart could be beyond comprehension. To avoid this situation, data flowcharts are structured in a parent–child relationship to show different levels of detail.

The structuring process is done by taking each individual process on the parent data flowchart and expanding it into its own child data flowchart. The rules stated above apply for drawing the parent and child data flowcharts, but there are some additional rules.

First, the net data flows between the parent and the child charts must match and their names must be the same. If the parent process has one input and two outputs, the net data flows of the child chart must be one input and two outputs.

Second, data storages are shown on each data flowchart where they are used. Data flows to and from data storages cannot be net data flows because they are not named. Therefore, the data storage must be shown on both the parent and child data flowcharts.

Even in a database environment where the logical view name appears on the data flow, the storage is still shown on each data flowchart. This is done because the name of the logical view may not clearly indicate the name of the data storage.

Figure 2.20 shows the data flowchart of a total system (System X) as one process with the net inputs and outputs of the system. This is the parent data flowchart.

The child data flowchart shown in Figure 2.21 shows the major processes in System X, making sure that the net data flows balance. The parent data flowchart of System X shows two inputs and one output. The child data flowchart also shows two inputs (Data Flows 1 and 2) and one output (Data Flow 3), and the data flow names match the parent data flow chart.

Figure 2.20 Overview data flowchart of a system.

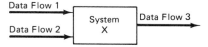

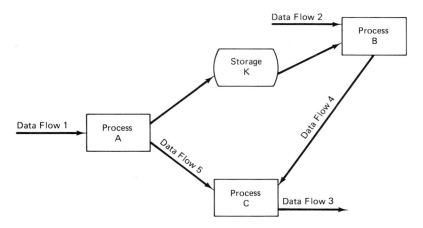

Figure 2.21   Child data flowchart showing major components of a system.

The next level of detail could have three separate child data flowcharts, one for each of the three parent processes (A, B, and C). The child data flowchart for Process C is shown in Figure 2.22. The net data flows and data flow names match the parent Process C in Figure 2.21.

Figure 2.21 contains a Data Storage K and Figure 2.22 contains a Data Storage L. These are two separate data storages and have no relation to each other. The different data storage names indicate this difference.

The child data flowchart for Process B is shown in Figure 2.23. Data Storage K is shown in this chart as it is shown in the parent data flowchart in Figure 2.21. Data storage K is considered as a net data flow. Thus both the parent and the child have two net inputs (Data Flow 2 and Storage K) and one net output (Data Flow 4).

Naming processes, storages, and data flows is up to the individual organization. Generally, a letter or number combination is used to denote the hierarchy, followed by a literal that uniquely defines the process, storage, or data flow. This combination gives a ready cross-reference, as well as a title that uniquely describes the processing or data.

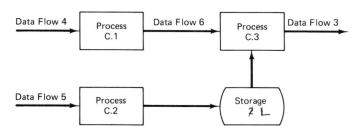

Figure 2.22   Detailed data flowchart for Process C.

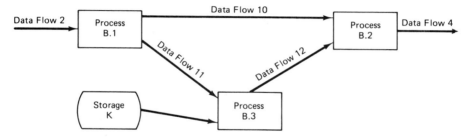

Figure 2.23   Detailed data flowchart for Process B.

As data flowcharts are defined in greater detail, a point is reached where it is not beneficial to develop more detailed data flowcharts. That point occurs when there are no new data flows being defined, when all the data storages are identified, and when a process cannot be reasonably divided to reduce further the number of inputs and outputs. At this point the lowest-level data flowchart has been developed.

When looking at a process to determine if a child data flowchart should be developed, there are six criteria to consider.

1. Are there any data storages that have not been defined?
2. Are there any data flows that have not been defined?
3. Are there subprocesses that occur at different times?
4. Are there subprocesses that occur at different locations?
5. Have the number of data flows been reduced to a reasonable minimum?
6. Are there subprocesses performed by different people or different units?

If the answer to one or more of these criteria is positive, a detail data flowchart should be developed.

Once the data flows, storages, and processes are defined, data structure charts are prepared for each unique data flow on the data flowchart. If the data flows have different structures, a data structure chart is prepared. If the data flow has different contents or is only a change of knowledge about the data, a separate data structure chart is not prepared.

Data flowcharts are a tool for identifying all the processes, data storages, and data flows in a system. They provide a method of structuring data and processes from a simple overview of the system to the greatest detail necessary without creating confusion. The result is a set of detailed data flowcharts that are used to design and develop the system further.

DATA RELATIONS

When developing data structures and designing databases, it is important to know how data are related to each other. Entities, attributes, and values have already been defined, with entities being the subject for defining subject databases. Data relations are the relationships between entities.

One-to-One Relation

The simplest data relation is one-to-one, where two entities are mutually unique; i.e., an occurrence in one entity is related to only one occurrence in the other. A good example is boat registration number. Only one boat registration number exists for any individual fishing boat, and a unique fishing boat has only one boat registration number. The relation is one fishing boat to one boat registration number. A one-to-one relationship is shown by placing Boat Registration Number as an attribute for the entity Fishing Boat, as shown in Figure 2.24.

The same situation exists if there is only one operator for each fishing boat and each operator works on only one fishing boat. The operator characteristics, e.g., name, height, weight, and birth date, could be attributes for Fishing Boat, as shown in Figure 2.25.

It is equally correct in a one-to-one relationship to show fishing boat characteristics as attributes for operator since the entities Fishing Boat and Operator are mutually unique. To avoid any confusion an entity name that describes the entity correctly must be used, such as Operational Fishing Boat.

One-to-Many Relation

The next data relation is a one-to-many or a many-to-one relation. For instance, if there are many operators for one fishing boat, i.e., to keep the boat operating 24 hours a day, seven days a week, but each operator works on only one fishing boat, there would be a relation of many operators to one boat, and one fishing boat with many operators.

This data relation is shown structurally as one fishing boat with many operators; i.e., the entity with many occurrences is subordinate to the entity with one occurrence. In Figure 2.26, operator is subordinate to fishing boat. The characteristics unique to fishing boat are listed as attributes within the

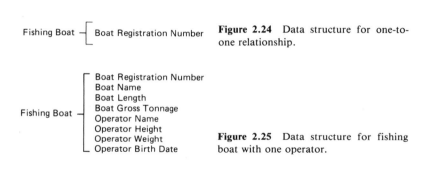

Fishing Boat — Boat Registration Number

Figure 2.24 Data structure for one-to-one relationship.

Fishing Boat —
Boat Registration Number
Boat Name
Boat Length
Boat Gross Tonnage
Operator Name
Operator Height
Operator Weight
Operator Birth Date

Figure 2.25 Data structure for fishing boat with one operator.

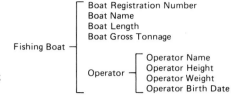

Figure 2.26 Data structure for fishing boat with many operators.

Fishing Boat set. The characteristics unique to operator are listed as attributes within the Operator set.

Many-to-Many Relation

The third data relation is a many-to-many relation. For instance, if there are many operators for one fishing boat, and any one operator may work on many fishing boats, there is a many-to-many relation. This relation can be shown structurally both as operators for each Fishing Boat as in Figure 2.26, and as Fishing Boats for each Operator as in Figure 2.27.

Inverted Data Relation

An inverted data structure shows the relation between one attribute and its related attributes. An attribute is designated as a data group and other attributes are used to characterize that data group. For instance, to show fishing boats by gross tonnage class requires the one-to-many data structure shown in Figure 2.28.

Since the fishing boat data already exists, only the key to that fishing boat is needed, i.e., Boat Registration Number. The data structure can be reduced to the one shown in Figure 2.29, which is a one-to-many relation

Figure 2.27 Data structure for fishing boats and operators in a many-to-many relation.

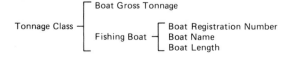

Figure 2.28 Data structure for fishing boats by tonnage class.

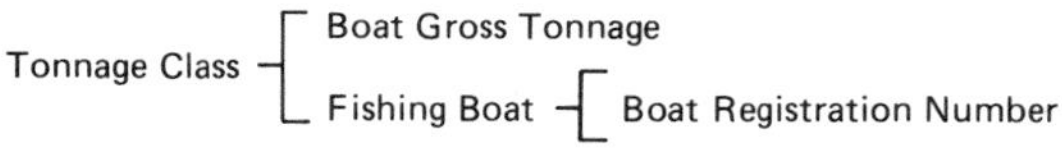

```
                    ┌─ Boat Gross Tonnage
  Tonnage Class ─┤
                    └─ Fishing Boat ─┤ Boat Registration Number
```

Figure 2.29   Data structure for inverted tonnage class list.

where fishing boat contains only the Boat Registration Number. This data structure becomes an inverted list.

Inverted lists can be created for any attribute in a data structure, giving any attribute the capability of being designated as a data group. This concept, plus an understanding of the three types of data relations, provides the basic knowledge for designing databases.

A basic knowledge of data relations is necessary to develop accurate data structures. If data structures are not accurate, the resulting process logic and subject databases will not be accurate. Therefore, a working knowledge of data relations and data structures is of critical importance to successful systems.

DATA NAMES

Data is the substance of data processing, and correct data names are crucial for successful data processing. A system can fail to be successful because of something as subtle as inappropriate data names. Therefore, each attribute must be studied, evaluated, and correctly named to provide a solid foundation for successful data processing.

Corporate data management emphasizes corporate-wide management and control of the data resource. Data names are an all-important part of the data and must be a primary consideration in data resource management. In fact, good data resource management must begin with good data names.

The relational database environment is based on the grouping of data by subject and the definition of relations between those subjects. It is not based on relations between business applications or the relation between the business application and the subject data. The applications data requirements are secondary to the management of subject databases.

Data independence is another primary consideration of data resource management. Subject databases are developed and maintained independent of the business applications that access those databases. Since the emphasis is on management of the subject databases, not on the business applications, the data must be named relative to its subject, not to the application.

Data names must be unique, descriptive, meaningful, and understandable. The process of naming data is not easy, but it must be done to have successful subject databases and successful applications. It requires considerable thought and evaluation from both the user and data processing personnel.

Data names must be defined in parallel with system development. They cannot be defined out of context with system design, i.e., before or after system design. To do so creates improper names and increases the risk of synonyms, homonyms, and data redundancy.

A well-designed database has controlled redundancy and no synonyms or homonyms. Each attribute is defined uniquely only once and redundancy is limited to relations between subject databases. This is the most productive database and helps assure a successful application.

Entity Names

A data entity is a person, place, thing, or event as defined earlier and becomes a subject in a relational database environment. Each entity must have a name that indicates that subject. This entity name may be one word, or several words, uniquely identifying the data entity within the entire company.

Data entities can be identified in two ways. The first and most important is the business entity model developed during system design. This model shows the business entities with which the company deals and the transactions between those entities.

A simple business entity model with three business entities and four transactions between those entities is shown in Figure 2.30. Employers pay Wages to Employees and make Premium Payments to the Insurance Company. Employees file Insurance Claims to the Insurance Company and receive Benefit Payments from the Insurance Company.

Each of these business entities and the transactions between them become a separate data entity. Each data entity contains a unique set of attributes describing that entity. Each of these data entities becomes a potential subject in the relational database environment.

Each data entity on a business entity model must be unique and must have a unique name. As the model is expanded this uniqueness must be maintained. Any time that the same name appears more than once, the situation must be reviewed and resolved before design continues.

The second way to identify data entities is with data structures. Data

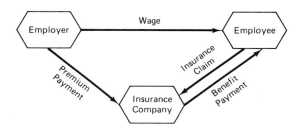

Figure 2.30   Business entity model for an insurance company.

structures are developed for each data flow on a data flow chart. The set labels for each set of data in a data structure is the data entity name.

Some of these data entities will already have been identified on the business entity model. However, there may be additional data entities required for processing that do not appear on the model. These additional entities are just as important as those on the business entity model.

The uniqueness of data entities must be maintained between those identified on the business entity model and those identified on data structures. It is not important whether those data entities ever appear on a database. It is important that each data entity be unique within the entire company.

A list of data entity names should be maintained and updated as new data entities are identified. This list helps designers identify new and existing entities and name them correctly.

One of the worst things to do is to guess entity names without benefit of business entity models or data structures. This inevitably leads to the wrong entity name and to nonunique entity names. These incorrect names are propagated through the entire design and development process and ultimately reduce productivity.

Another poor practice is to identify all data entities prior to design. These entities are inevitably either subsets of true data entities or data groups that cross data entity boundaries. The impact of this practice is more severe than the impact of incorrect data entity names.

Frequently, data entities are named by the system, or program, that uses them or the physical file where they are stored. This practice is a result of traditional file-processing techniques and is wrong in the database environment. Data must be grouped and named by subject, not by how they are physically stored or used.

The only sure way to identify and name data entities properly is to define data in parallel with system development. Business entity models and data structures are the best source for identifying data entity names. A list of valid, unique data entity names based on entity models and data structures developed during system design assures a stable database and a successful system.

Attribute Names

Attributes are qualifiers that characterize or describe an entity. The attribute name follows the entity name. Together they form the complete attribute name.

Each attribute must have a data entity name. If there is no entity name, it is very difficult to know what subject the attribute characterizes. Lack of an entity name also leads to synonyms, homonyms, and data redundancy.

Attribute names should consist of meaningful words that describe the attribute and make it unique. Prepositions, connectives, and meaningless words should not be used. They make the attribute name longer than necessary and add nothing to the clarity of the name.

The "Of Language," popular several years ago, should not be used. It was used to name attributes from the attribute detail level to the entity, separating each work with "of," i.e., Data Of Birth Of Employee. It is far better, and more meaningful, to use the name Employee Birth Date.

One exception to the entity name on each attribute occurs on data structures. For simplicity and clarity the entity name is sometimes omitted, but it is implied by the name of the set containing the attribute. When the attribute is removed from the set it must be prefixed with the name of the set.

Figure 2.31 shows a data structure with implied entity names. The Name, Account Number, and Total Wage Dollars within the Employer set are really Employer Name, Employer Account Number, and Employer Total Wage Dollars. The same is true for the Employee set. A decimal point is inserted in front of these truncated data item names to indicate that the entity name is implied.

Multiple entity names cannot be used in an attribute name. A frequent mistake is to use multiple entity names in an attribute name, particularly for transactions. These multiple entity names cause extreme difficulty in understanding what the attribute represents.

The business entity model in Figure 2.30 shows a wage transaction from employer to employee. The data entity name for this transaction is Wage. It is not Employer Wage, Employee Wage, or even Employer Employee Wage. Its name is simply Wage, to designate the set of data moving from Employer to Employee.

One apparent exception to multiple entity names appears with indicators. For instance, an employer makes multiple tax payments to the government, so both employer and tax payment are data entities. However, the due date for the tax payment is different for each employer and is part of the employer data set. The attribute name is Employer Tax Payment Due Date.

This is not an exception to the multiple-entity-name rule because the data entity is Employer and the attribute name is Tax Payment Due Date. The data entity is not Employer Tax Payment. This distinction must be kept clear when naming attributes.

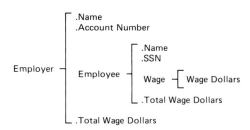

Figure 2.31 Implied entity names on attributes in a data structure.

Data Name Examples

To illustrate further the naming of attributes, good and bad examples will be shown and explained. A common mistake in naming attributes is to confuse codes and descriptions. For instance, Employer Class has both a code and a description. The attribute names should be Employer Class Code and Employer Class Description.

An attribute named Employer Class Code Description is not valid. It is not clear if the attribute is a code, or a description, or both. Nor is it clear if it is the description of the code (not the code value) or of Employer Class.

A similar mistake is to have two attributes that are not explicit. For instance, there are two attributes for a full description and an abbreviated description named Department Description and Department Abbreviated Description. To make them explicit, these names should be Department Full Description and Department Abbreviated Description.

Another common mistake is to use the same attribute to indicate more than one characteristic. For instance, employers report the number of hours actually worked during the month for each employee. This number can range from zero to an absolute maximum of 744.

If the number is reported by the employer, it is stored as Employee Monthly Wage Hours. If it is not reported, it is calculated by either of two methods. If it is calculated by method 1, it is stored in Employee Monthly Wage Hours as 1000 plus the number of hours. If it is calculated by method 2, it is stored in Employee Monthly Wage Hours as 2000 plus the number of hours. In other words, the first digit is how the hours were obtained and the next three digits are the actual hours.

This attribute should actually be two attributes. Employee Monthly Wage Hours should contain the actual hours however they were obtained. Employee Monthly Wage Indicator should indicate how the wage hours were obtained.

Another common problem is the same attribute that appears in multiple entities. For instance, a company has many employees, including auditors, terminal operators, and interviewers. When defining attributes the identification code for each employee might be defined separately for each entity. Thus there could be Audit Auditor ID, Tax Payment Terminal Operator, and Client Interviewer Code attributes.

Each of these attributes contains the six-digit organizational identification code for the employee, commonly referred to as Staff ID. Staff ID is unique to a specific employee in a specific job. Management reports are produced for each employee based on Staff ID.

The data structure for the management reports contains the attribute Staff ID, yet the Audit, Tax Payment, and Client entities contain their respective attribute names. This creates synonomous data attributes, which if unresolved, could create a design problem and cause excessive coding.

The problem is resolved by establishing Staff as a data entity which could ultimately contain information about each person on the staff, such as name, ID, birth date, sex, etc. Staff ID becomes the correct attribute name which is used in the Audit, Tax Payment, and Client entities.

Therefore, the same attribute could appear in multiple entities. That attribute will not have the entity name of the entity where it appears, but will have its own entity name. These attributes are actually foreign keys to their own entity, which will be explained later.

The reverse situation can occur when an attribute is not specific to an entity. For instance, Transaction Code appears in the Tax Payment, Wage, and Employer entities. However, these transaction code values and meanings are different for each of these entities. Even if they are not different initially, there is a high probability that they will be different in the future.

This situation is resolved by specifically naming each attribute with its respective entity. This produces Tax Payment Transaction Code, Wage Transaction Code, and Employer Transaction Code. Now the values of these codes can change based on the needs of the entity they belong to without consideration of transaction codes in other entities.

In some situations the subject entity names are not the same as the name of the data set that contains the attributes. For instance, wage data is being entered and edited. Good data will go to the Wage storage and data with errors will go the Wage Suspense storage, as shown in Figure 2.32.

The data structures for the Wage and Wage Suspense data storages are shown in Figure 2.33. The Wage entity attributes all begin with the entity name Wage, except the foreign keys to Employer and Employee. The Wage Suspense entity attributes, however, contain a variety of entity names.

Wage Suspense Batch Number identifies the Wage Suspense data. Employee Name is used to verify Employee SSN if it is in error. Staff ID is the person entering wage data and Wage Error is the explanation of any errors. These attributes are used for correcting errors and do not go to the Wage Storage.

The entity name of an attribute is the basic subject of the data regardless of any interim stages that data passes through. The data in Wage Suspense is basic wage data and, therefore, carries the entity name Wage. The Wage Suspense storage is an interim step in the process of putting good wages in the Wage storage.

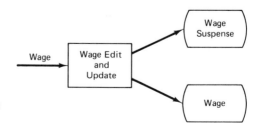

Figure 2.32   Wage data editing with wage and wage suspense storages.

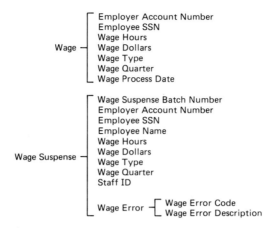

Figure 2.33   Data structures for wage and wage suspense storages.

The same reasoning is true for a transaction file carrying extracts of various subjects for a report generator, or a storage of audit trail data from various entities. It would be ridiculous to rename each attribute to match each data set containing that data. This would create monumental attribute name synonyms.

Another problem that occurs is separate data entities that apparently represent the same basic subject. For instance, an employee is working and receiving wages. However, should this person become unemployed he or she is a claimant seeking unemployment payments based on the wages that he or she earned as an employee.

Even though the claimant and employee is the same person, the set of data for that person as an employee is different from the set of data for that person as a claimant. A few data items may be similar, such as SSN, name, birth date, etc., but the two sets of data are distinctly different. Therefore, there are two different entities: one for employee and one for claimant.

The worst thing to do in this situation is to create one entity, say Client, for all attributes from both employee and claimant. Although this fits the client as a person, it confuses the use of subject data. The subjects in this case are Employees who are working and Claimants who are receiving unemployment payments.

The attributes common to both sets of data could be put into a separate entity for the person. That entity would then contain attributes that were pertinent to both the employee and claimant entities. This would reduce the data redundancy without confusing the subjects of employee and claimant.

A similar problem occurs when the same attributes are defined with different names in different entities. For instance, data is defined for a customer, such as name, address, phone, etc., and data is defined for warranties, orders, and payment contracts, which pertain to customers. The error occurs when attributes are defined for Warranty Customer Name, Order Customer Name, Contract Customer Name, etc.

Customer attributes must be placed in a customer entity while warranty, order, and payment contract attributes are placed in their respective entities. The relation between these entities is then defined to allow customer attributes to be applicable to warranties, orders, and payments.

The naming of attributes requires constant study and evaluation to place them in the correct entities and name them properly. When the attributes are analyzed and named properly, the subject databases will be correct and processing applications will operate efficiently.

Managing Data Names

The management and control of attribute names is the responsibility of a data administration unit. That unit should have the authority to establish, accept, or reject data names, and to establish and enforce standards for naming data. That unit must coordinate the naming and use of data throughout the entire company.

One important standard to be established and strictly enforced is the use of abbreviations. A list of standard abbreviations must be maintained and any abbreviation that is contrary to that list must be corrected or rejected.

There are two basic rules for abbreviation. First is the abbreviation for each word in an attribute name. Regardless of the specific rule for abbreviating a word, which is up to the individual organization, the abbreviation must substantially shorten the word, yet maintain its meaning. Where possible, commonly known abbreviations should be used.

Generally, it is a poor practice to abbreviate a string of words to the first letter of each word. Exceptions to this rule are widely known and used phrases, which should always be abbreviated to the first letter of each word. For instance, abbreviating Monthly Wage Total to MWT would be meaningless to most people. However, OASI is a common abbreviation of Old Age and Survivors' Insurance and should always be used. The list of abbreviations should indicate these mandatory abbreviations.

Second is the sequence of abbreviating the words in a data item name, i.e., right to left or left to right. Either direction is appropriate and equally useful, and it is not important which sequence is used. What is important is that the sequence be standard for the organization so that everyone is abbreviating a name the same way.

The objectives for establishing abbreviation rules are to produce shorter, meaningful names, to prevent synonyms and homonyms, and to provide easy look-up in a data dictionary. When abbreviation rules are not followed, meaningless and synonymous names are created, redundancy increases, and data name reference becomes time consuming. The result is decreased productivity.

A data dictionary must be used to manage attribute names and descriptions. This dictionary can be as simple as 3 by 5 index cards or a fully automated data dictionary and directory system. The physical form is not important, but the use of some form of data dictionary is extremely important.

Most data dictionaries have the ability to include one primary attribute name and multiple aliases. The primary name should be the fully spelled out, real-world, logical attribute name. All other forms of that name, i.e., abbreviated name, source code name, etc., should be aliases of the primary name.

Data names must be managed to provide a stable foundation for subject databases and the use of that data by processing applications. Even though the changing business environment causes changes in data names, these changes should be minimized. The establishment of good attribute names initially means that name changes can be limited to those resulting from the changing business environment.

Data-Naming Rules

Naming data is an important step in defining subject data and preventing redundancy. A few rules have been described for naming data. A detailed list of data-naming rules is presented below.

1. An entity name must be unique, descriptive, and meaningful.
2. An entity name may represent either subject entities or transaction entities.
3. An entity name must be fully qualified and unique within the company.
4. Entity names are identified from business entity models and from data structures.
5. An attribute is the smallest unit of information.
6. A single attribute must not contain two or more pieces of information.
7. An attribute name must be unique, descriptive, and meaningful.
8. An attribute name consists of the entity name first, followed by the attribute name.
9. An entity name must be used in the attribute name.
10. Multiple entity names will not be used in an attribute name.
11. All qualifiers go at the end of an attribute name.
12. Prepositions and connectives will not be used in attribute names.
13. The "Of Language" will not be used to name attributes.
14. Attribute numbers will not be used in place of attribute names.
15. The primary attribute name is the real-world name, fully qualified and fully spelled out.
16. All other variations, including abbreviations, are defined as aliases.
17. Abbreviations must be meaningful.

18. Abbreviations must result in substantial length reductions.
19. Words with three letters or less are not abbreviated.
20. Mandatory abbreviations should be identified on the abbreviation list.
21. The sequence of abbreviations, i.e., right to left or left to right, must be specified.
22. Abbreviate all manifestations of a root word.
23. Abbreviations using the first letter of each word are used only when it is well known.
24. A central authority, i.e., Data Administration, will establish standards and control the naming of data.
25. A data dictionary must be available, regardless of its form.

Data item names are important for a successful database environment and successful systems. Poor data names decrease the chances for a successful system, while good data names increase the chances for a successful system. Therefore, each attribute must be studied, evaluated, and named according to formal standards to provide a solid foundation for successful systems.

ENTITY KEYS

Keys are attributes that have special use in addition to the values they contain for describing an entity. They are used to identify uniquely each occurrence in an entity and to navigate from one entity to another in a relational database environment. Without the availability of properly designated keys there cannot be a truly functional database environment.

Primary Key

Each entity must have an attribute as a primary key that will uniquely identify each occurrence in that entity. This primary key must have a different value for each occurrence in the entity. No two occurrences in an entity can have the same value in their primary key or, by definition, it is not a true primary key.

A primary key must also be nonredundant. No part of the key can be removed without destroying the uniqueness of the key for identifying each occurrence in the entity. If there is a redundant value in the primary key, then by definition, it is not a true primary key.

In the section on data names it was emphasized that only one characteristic is contained in an attribute. If this rule is followed, a single attribute used as a primary key cannot contain a value that is redundant for use as a key. It is only when a single attribute contains more than one characteristic that it has the potential for being redundant as a primary key.

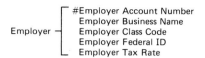

Figure 2.34 Primary key for identifying a unique employer.

Primary keys also provide access to the occurrences in an entity. When a unique occurrence is sought, the primary key is used to locate and obtain that occurrence. If the primary key were not unique, multiple occurrences would be obtained, resulting in unnecessary processing.

A primary key is designated with a pound sign (#) in front of the attribute name. Figure 2.34 shows a data structure for employer data. Each employer is uniquely identified by Employer Account Number as the primary key.

Access to a unique occurrence in the employer entity is made with the Employer Account Number. No single number can be assigned to two or more employers. This criterion becomes part of the assignment process or edit process and must be enforced to maintain Employer Account Number as a true primary key.

Secondary Key

A secondary key is an attribute that is used for accessing occurrences in an entity but is not necessary for uniquely identifying that occurrence. More than one occurrence in an entity can have that same value for its secondary key, and there may be more than one secondary key in an entity. The purpose of secondary keys is to obtain a group of occurrences with the same characteristic.

A secondary key is designated with a minus sign (-) in front of the attribute name. Figure 2.35 shows a data structure for employee data. Each employee is uniquely identified with Employee SSN as the primary key. In addition, Employee Job Title is identified as a secondary key.

Employee Job Title is used to obtain all employees with a specific job title. For instance, if there were 22 occurrences in the employee entity with a job title of Master Mechanic, 22 occurrences would be obtained with a secondary key value of Master Mechanic.

Foreign Key

A foreign key is the primary key of one entity that is placed in a second entity for the purpose of accessing the first entity. Foreign keys are used to

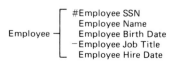

Figure 2.35 Secondary key for accessing employee data.

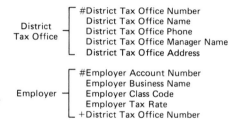

```
                              ┌ #District Tax Office Number
                              │  District Tax Office Name
              District        │  District Tax Office Phone
             Tax Office  ─────┤  District Tax Office Manager Name
                              └  District Tax Office Address

                              ┌ #Employer Account Number
                              │  Employer Business Name
              Employer  ──────┤  Employer Class Code
                              │  Employer Tax Rate
                              └ +District Tax Office Number
```

Figure 2.36 Foreign key from employer to district tax office.

navigate between entities in a relational database. Without foreign keys there would be no method to navigate readily between entities.

A foreign key is designated with a plus sign (+) in front of the attribute name. Figure 2.36 shows data structures for District Tax Office and Employer. Each tax office has many employers that it regulates, and each employer is regulated by only one tax office.

The primary key for district tax office is District Tax Office Number. Since an employer is regulated by only one tax office, the District Tax Office Number is carried as a foreign key in the employer entity. When any data about the tax office for an employer is required, the appropriate tax office occurrence is accessed and the required data is obtained.

Compound Key

In some situations a single attribute will not uniquely identify each occurrence in an entity. Several attributes may be necessary for the unique identification of each occurrence. This group of attributes is called a compound key, as opposed to a single attribute in a primary key.

All attributes forming a compound key are designated with a pound sign (#), the same as a primary key. The only difference is that there are two or more attributes designated for an entity. Figure 2.37 shows the data structure for a legal document with a compound key.

Each legal document has a Document Number; however, the Document Number is not unique for each type of legal document processed. The same document number may appear on different types of legal documents. Therefore, both Document Type Code and Document Number must be used as a compound key.

However, these two attributes do not form a true compound key because they do not uniquely identify legal documents between counties. Document County Code must be added to the compound key. These three attributes form a true compound key that makes each legal document unique.

```
                              ┌ #Document Number
                              │ #Document Type Code
           Legal Document  ───┤ #Document County Code
                              │  Document Issue Date
                              └  Document Release Date
```

Figure 2.37 Compound key for uniquely identifying a legal document.

Composite Key

A similar situation occurs when attributes from another entity are required to identify uniquely an occurrence in one entity. This group of attributes is termed a composite key. Composite keys are usually needed to identify uniquely accumulated data that is stored.

Figure 2.38 shows a data structure for yearly wage hours and dollars for each employee for each employer that employee worked for, and a data structure for yearly wage hours and dollars for each employee for each county where that employee worked. Even though the attribute names are Year Hours and Year Dollars on each chart, they are clearly not the same attributes. They are different because the hierarchy above the Year entity is different.

Since these yearly wages were accumulated in two different hierarchies, they belong to two different entities with different composite keys. The first yearly accumulation needs a composite key of Employer Account Number, Employee SSN, and Calendar Year. The second yearly accumulation needs a composite key of County Code, Employee SSN, and Calendar Year.

Neither entity could use a composite of just Employee SSN and Calendar Year because the first is accumulated by employer and the second is accumulated by county. The primary key of each entity in the hierarchy above the accumulated attribute must be used to make a unique composite key. Even if the highest entities are identical, all the primary keys must still be used as a composite key because there is no guarantee the hierarchies will be identical in the future.

The situation shown in Figure 2.38 often escapes detection until late in testing or implementation. This occurs because the entities and attributes are

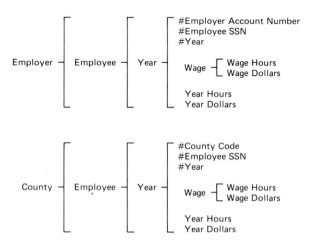

Figure 2.38 Composite key for uniquely identifying accumulated wage data.

not properly named. It would be easy in this example to leave the entity name as Year with attributes Year Hours and Year Dollars and a primary key of Calendar Year. However, the data would not be correct.

It is better to define each attribute explicitly and verify its use. If this were done, it is clear that the two Year entities are different. Once they are known to be different, they can be named appropriately and the correct composite keys can be identified.

Choosing Keys

When choosing an attribute as a primary key, there are three simple rules to follow. First, that attribute must make each occurrence in the entity unique. If that attribute does not make each occurrence unique, a different attribute must be used or a compound key must be used.

Second, if a compound key is used, the attributes must not be redundant. If one or more attributes could be left out and uniqueness maintained, then there are too many attributes in the compound key. One or more attributes must be dropped until there is no redundancy, yet uniqueness is maintained.

If a compound key contains more than three attributes to achieve uniqueness, an arbitrary attribute should be created as a primary key. This arbitrary attribute could be manually assigned, computer assigned, or derived from other attributes. The source of the arbitrary attribute is unimportant as long as a single primary key is identified.

Third, if there is a choice of attributes for a primary key or compound key, the attribute that is shortest or numeric should be selected. For instance, if both Customer Account Number (five-digit numeric) and Customer Name (24-digit alpha) were unique, the account number should be chosen because it is both shorter and numeric.

Keys are used to identify unique occurrences in an entity and to navigate between entities in a relational database environment. The proper identification and use of keys is important to both unique identification and navigation and leads to effective and efficient use of the database. Any database built in this manner will increase the productivity of both the data-processing staff and the end user.

SUMMARY

Traditional processing was based on physical records and physical files that were application specific. This type of processing led to physical constraints, limited scope of design, and limited user involvement. This resulted in ineffective and inefficient systems.

Data-structured processes and data-structured databases are based on the structure of data flowing in the system. Data flowcharts are developed to show the architecture of the processes, storages, and the data flows. Data structures are then developed for each unique data flow and are used to define both process logic and subject databases.

These data structures show the relation between data entities and the data attributes contained within each entity. Both entities and attributes are specifically named to prevent data synonyms and homonyms, and data redundancy. Entity keys are identified on data structures to identify each occurrence in an entity uniquely and to navigate between entities.

The data-structured approach provides a database that meets the needs of all applications, yet has minimum redundancy and maximum flexibility for future changes. It also provides applications that are structured according to the data and can readily process that data. The result is systems that are more effective and efficient.

STUDY QUESTIONS

1. What are the disadvantages of a physically oriented design?
2. What is the purpose of data flowcharts?
3. How are data flowcharts modified for a database management system environment?
4. What are the criteria for developing a more detailed child data flowchart?
5. What is the difference between entities, attributes, and values?
6. What is being structured in a data structure?
7. What is the difference between one-to-one, one-to-many, and many-to-many relations?
8. What is an inverted data relation?
9. How are attributes named?
10. How are entity names identified?
11. What happens when attributes are not properly named?
12. What is the difference between a primary key, a composite key, and a compound key?
13. How do secondary keys and foreign keys differ from primary keys?
14. How are keys selected?
15. What are the advantages of the data-structured approach?

3

DATA STRUCTURES

When the architecture of a system has been defined on data flowcharts, data structures are prepared for each data flow. The process of preparing these data structures is termed *data structure composition*. The data is reviewed and analyzed and data structures are composed based on that analysis.

The outputs are reviewed and a data structure is prepared for each output exactly as it appears. For each output data structure a required data structure is composed showing exactly what is needed from the database, and how the database is accessed for that data. The same procedure is followed for inputs and their necessary data structures to access and maintain the database.

After data structures are composed, the required and necessary data structures are taken apart and rearranged to form the logical database. The process of taking data structures apart and forming the logical database is termed *data structure decomposition*. The result of decomposition is a logical database containing all the entities, their attributes, and access paths necessary to support the inputs and outputs defined during design.

The process of composing and decomposing data structures provides the ability to model the database before it is actually built. It also provides the ability to model any changes to the database before files are implemented. The result is a database that is structurally independent of specific applications, yet adequately supports many applications.

DATA STRUCTURE COMPOSITION

The development of data-structured databases is output driven with input verification. The outputs required to meet the user needs are used to develop the initial logical database. The inputs defined by the user provide a verification and possible refinement of the initial logical database.

The actual method of database design is described in Chapter 5. Briefly, there are four steps to producing a logical database. First, the outputs are analyzed to provide an output logical database which is used as the initial logical database.

Second, the inputs are analyzed to provide an input logical database. Third, the output and input logical databases are compared and adjusted until the logical structure and all attributes match. Fourth, the total logical database is developed from the combined inputs and outputs after they have been balanced.

The total logical database is used to build the physical database in a specific operating environment. The final logical database provides all the entities and attributes for developing an optimum physical database regardless of the specific database management system or the specific hardware. Any change in the physical environment needs only a change in the physical implementation, not a change in the total logical database.

The logical database is developed in parallel with application development. It cannot be done prior to application development because invalid assumptions are made and the grouping of attributes into proper data entities will probably be wrong. It cannot be done after application development because the application design becomes fixed on a very narrow scope of the total company database.

As data flowcharts are developed, the outputs and inputs are identified and defined. These outputs and inputs are analyzed and the resulting logical data storages are shown on the data flowcharts. As system design progresses, the data flowcharts represent the current perception of data flows, logic processing, and data storages.

Output Data Structures

Output data structures are developed for each output on the data flowcharts. These data structures represent the data as it is displayed on the actual output. They may or may not have any relation to the actual storage or retrieval of the data.

As each output is identified, the format of that output is defined and the output data structure is developed. It is not important whether the format or the data structure is actually developed first. It is important that both be developed together.

Several symbols are used on output data structures to identify the use of attributes. An at sign (@) is used to identify an attribute that is calculated or derived from other attributes. This attribute appears on the output but is not stored on the database. If an attribute is calculated or derived and is stored on the database, the at sign is not used.

An ampersand (&) is used to identify an attribute as a parameter that appears on the output but is entered at execution time. Parameters are not stored on the database. If a parameter is stored, the ampersand is not used and the appropriate parameter storage is identified.

A quote mark (') is used to identify an attribute containing a literal or constant that appears on the output but is not stored on the database. Literals and constants are stored in the program source code. If they are stored in the database, the quote mark is not used and the appropriate literal storage is defined.

If there is no symbol prefixing an attribute, that attribute appears on the output and is stored on the database. Occasionally, output data structures are developed where the status of an attribute is uncertain. A question mark (?) is used to indicate this uncertainty. All uncertainties must be resolved before an output data structure can become final.

A Vehicle Report designed to meet a user's specific needs is shown in Figure 3.1. It shows the mileage driven and job identification for vehicles and

REPORT 143X	ACE COMPANY VEHICLE REPORT			JUNE 20, 19xx	
Division Name	Section Name	Operator Name	Vehicle License	Job ID	Miles Driven
Administration	Fiscal	Smith	R14569	A432	123
		Wilson	R14325	A602	468
			X44623	A602	96
		Jones	X54789	A103	102
			P44938	A498	84
	Fiscal Total				873
	Personnel	Jackson	R98756	A236	82
		Williams	R56923	A301	106
	Personnel Total				188
Administration Total					1061
Construction		Burke	K87640	C406	498
	Field	Paulson	D54983	C406	672
	Field Total				1170
Construction Total					1170
Company Total					2231

Figure 3.1 Output format for a vehicle report.

operators of each section and division within the company. Totals are shown for vehicle, operator, section, division, and company.

The data structure for this report, shown in Figure 3.2, is relatively easy to compose. There is only one Company, so it becomes the highest entity in the structure. The highest entity in any data structure must be a single-occurrence entity. If it is not, the highest entity has not been identified, and must be identified before the data structure is complete.

Within the company there are multiple divisions forming a one-to-many relation between Company and Division. Remember, the entity with many occurrences is subordinate to the entity with one occurrence. Therefore, Division is a subentity of Company.

The same relation exists for Section within Division, Operator within Section, and Vehicle within Operator. If it is unclear from the output what the data structure is, the data must be carefully analyzed to determine which entity occurs multiple times for one occurrence of another entity. When this has been determined the data structure can be composed.

Division, section, and operator names are shown at the top of their respective data sets. The attributes in the Vehicle set are Vehicle License, Job Identification, and Vehicle Miles. The accumulated mileages are shown at the bottom of their respective data sets.

The attributes for company are identified as literals. The attributes for accumulated miles are identified as calculated. The use of these identifiers is explained further in the following section.

The statistical report shown in Figure 3.3 is a typical table for fish landings with species of fish listed horizontally and fishing boats listed vertically. Totals are shown at the right for each boat and at the bottom for each species. The company total is shown at the lower right.

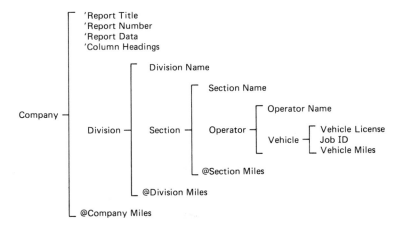

Figure 3.2 Output data structure for vehicle report.

REPORT 7892	AMBO COMPANY FISH LANDINGS Pounds By Species				JUNE 29, 19xx
Boat Name	Salmon	Tuna	Flounder	Other	Boat Pounds
Mary K	1436				1436
Bertha		2968	1628		4596
Solitude				4233	4233
Rover		1982		941	2923
Catchem	4876				4876
Species Pounds	6312	4950	1628	5174	18064

Figure 3.3 Output format for report of fish landings.

The data structure for this report, shown in Figure 3.4, is a little more difficult to compose. There is a one-to-many relation between Company and Boat, and between Company and Species. There is also a one-to-many relation between Boat and Species. This situation is common in reports with crossfoot totals.

Pounds are shown for each species for each boat. Pounds are also shown for each boat with all species combined, and for each species with all boats combined. Company pounds is the grand total for all boats and all species. These attributes are placed within their respective sets.

The attributes for company are identified as literals. The attributes for accumulated pounds are identified as calculated.

Required Data Structures

Output data structures represent the structure of the data as it actually appears on the output. After the output data structure is developed, a required data structure is prepared for each output. This required data structure shows the structure of the data required from the database to support the output.

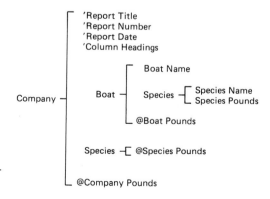

Figure 3.4 Output data structure for report of fish landings.

A required data structure is developed for each output data structure. It may be developed concurrently with the output data structure, or it may be developed after the output data structure is final. Either way is acceptable, but a required data structure must be developed for each output.

Required data structures are also developed for any other internal requirements from the database that do not have output formats or output data structures. These internal requirements must be identified to assure that internal databases are properly defined.

Several symbols are used on required data structures to identify the use of attributes. Primary, foreign, and secondary keys (explained in the section "Entity Keys") can appear on the required data structures.

An equal sign (=) is used to identify an attribute that is stored on the database and is needed to support the output, but does not appear on the output. These attributes are generally used in calculations. If the attribute appears on the output, an equal sign is not used.

If the status of an attribute is uncertain, a question mark (?) is used, the same as on the output data structures. All uncertainties must be resolved before the required data structure can become final.

The output data structure for the Vehicle Report was shown in Figure 3.2. The required data structure for that report is shown in Figure 3.5. The attributes identified as literal and calculated have been dropped because they are not required from the database. Division Name, Section Name, Operator Name, and Vehicle License have been identified as primary keys for their respective entities.

This required data structure shows the data required from the database for four entities. Three of these entities have only primary keys. The fourth entity has a primary key and two additional attributes. Company is still shown as the highest entity even though there is no data required from the database.

The output data for the fish landing report was shown in Figure 3.4. The required data structure is shown in Figure 3.6. The attributes identified as literals have been dropped, and primary keys have been identified for boat and species. The species entity within company has been dropped because there is no data required from the database.

The company entity is not dropped even though it has no required attributes because it is the highest single-occurrence entity. The required data

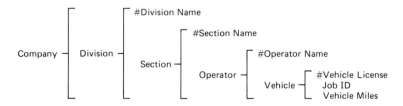

Figure 3.5   Required data structure for the vehicle report.

Figure 3.6 Required data structure for
fish landing report.

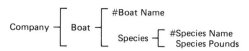

structure, like the output data structure, must have a single-occurrence entity as the highest entity. The species entity within company can be dropped because it is not the highest entity in the data structure and it does not have any required attributes.

Output and Required Data Structure Examples

The composition of correct output and required data structures is mandatory for accurate definition of databases. The examples above were simple and described the technique for developing data structures from outputs. Additional examples will be described to show the variety of situations that can occur. In these examples only the output and required data structures will be illustrated.

Usually, an attribute is displayed only once for each occurrence of an entity, i.e., Operator Name is displayed only once for each operator even though that operator drove several vehicles. However, in some situations an attribute may be displayed once for each occurrence of a subentity; i.e., Operator Name would be displayed once for each vehicle that operator drove.

The output data structure in Figure 3.7 shows that Operator Name is displayed once for each vehicle driven, not once for each operator. If the operator drove 12 vehicles during the reporting period, his or her name would appear 12 times on the report.

The required data structure is the same as that of Figure 3.5. Operator Name is moved from the vehicle entity to the operator entity because it changes only once per operator, not once per vehicle. The required data structure indicates the frequency with which an attribute changes, while the output data structure indicates the frequency with which an attribute is displayed.

Redundant attribute display may be acceptable to meet user needs. If an output shows an attribute once for each occurrence of its own entity, or once for each occurrence of a subentity, it is acceptable, and the required data structure will be identical. If an attribute is displayed once for each occurrence of a parent entity, there will be missing data and the output format must be changed.

Output data structures may have sets of data that represent data group-

Figure 3.7 Partial output data structure
for vehicle report with redundant display
of operator name.

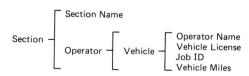

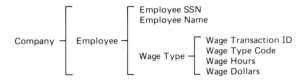

Figure 3.8 Output data structure for wage-type data list.

ings, not true subject entities. For instance, Figure 3.8 shows an output data structure for wage data by wage type for each employee in the company. If there were three types of wages paid to an employee, there would be three wage-type entries on the report.

The required data structure for the wage-type listing is shown in Figure 3.9. The Wage Type set has been changed to Wage since the subject entity is Wage. Employee SSN and Wage Transaction ID are identified as primary keys. Wage Type Code is not needed as a primary or compound key, but it is needed to group all occurrences of each wage type for an employee. Therefore, it is identified as a secondary key.

The procedure is to show the attribute used for grouping data as a data set on the output data structure. The required data structure shows the subject entity that attribute belongs to and shows that attribute within the entity. That attribute is identified as a secondary key unless it is already identified as a primary key.

This procedure applies whether one value of an attribute is selected, many values are selected, or all values are selected. The only change is the name of the data grouping on the output data structure, i.e., Wage Type, Wage Type 150, or Wage Types 150, 240, and 390. The required data structure is the same in each case.

Outputs that show aging of data provide another instance of data grouping. Figure 3.10 shows the output data structure for aging of delinquent accounts, i.e., 30 days, 60 days, and 90 days delinquent. The delinquency period is a literal, and both number of accounts delinquent and delinquent dollars are calculated.

The required data structure to produce the listing of aged delinquent accounts is shown in Figure 3.11. The Account Due Date and Account Amount Due are the only attributes required. The Account Due Date is identified as

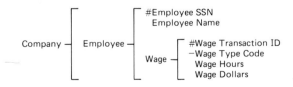

Figure 3.9 Required data structure for wage-type data list.

Figure 3.10 Output data structure for delinquent accounts.

Company ─┤ Delinquent Period ─┤ 'Delinquent Period @Delinquent Accounts @Delinquent Dollars

Figure 3.11 Required data structure for list of delinquent accounts.

Company ─┤ Account ─┤ −Account Due Date =Account Amount Due

a secondary key to retrieve delinquent account data. The Account Amount Due is identified as a supportive attribute because it is not listed on the output.

Some output processes are driven by transaction entities that are not displayed. Figure 3.12 shows the output data structure for a report of contract costs. The company has many contracts and each contract has many projects.

The required data structure in Figure 3.13 shows many tasks to be performed for each project. Task is the transaction entity that drives the output data structure, even though no task data appears on the output. Task contains the cost that is accumulated to the project and contract level.

The primary keys have been identified for Contract and Project. In the case of Task the Task ID is not unique; i.e., the same task may be performed for many projects, for many contracts. Therefore, a composite key of Contract Number, Project Code, and Task ID is needed to identify each task uniquely.

A transaction entity is the lowest-level subentity that drives an output data structure. Transaction entities do not have any subentities. If they do, they are not a true transaction entity.

In some situations an entity that is not a transaction entity is used to drive an output data structure. For instance, if a list of all projects for each contract were desired, the project entity would drive the output data structure. Only Project and Contract data are needed, so Task would not appear on either the output data structure or the required data structure.

Transaction entities frequently carry attributes to identify the parent entities above the transaction level. These attributes may not be a composite key if there is another primary key for each transaction. In many instances a primary key is not needed for transaction-level entities.

The output data structure for allocation of money to various projects and funds is shown in Figure 3.14. Allocations are transactions that move

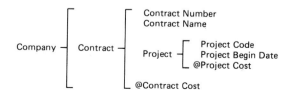

Figure 3.12 Output data structure for contract cost report.

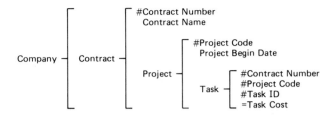

Figure 3.13   Required data structure for contract cost report.

money to and from various projects. A list of those transactions and current amounts is maintained for reference.

The required data structure for the allocation is shown in Figure 3.15. The primary keys are identified for Fund, Project, and Allocation. Fund Amount and Project Amount are stored on the database, so they are shown on the data structure. Fund Code and Project Code are also shown as attributes within the Allocation entity.

Another situation that may occur is a one-to-many relation that should be a one-to-one relation. A good example is Employee Name and Employee SSN, which should appear to be a one-to-one relation. However, there can be multiple names to one Employee SSN due to name changes.

An output data structure for all Employee Names that have the same Employee SSN and other attributes about that employee is shown in Figure 3.16. The Employee SSN and Employee Name data sets are data groupings, as explained earlier. They are not subject entities.

The required data structure is shown in Figure 3.17. Employee SSN is the designated primary key, although when multiple records are obtained it is not a true primary key.

A similar situation would be a list of multiple Employee SSNs for an Employee Name, with additional distinguishing attributes. This list could be useful for different people with identical names. Figure 3.18 shows the required data structure for this list. The primary key is still Employee SSN, but Employee Name has been identified as a secondary key.

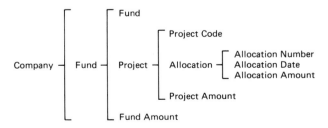

Figure 3.14   Output data structure for allocation of money.

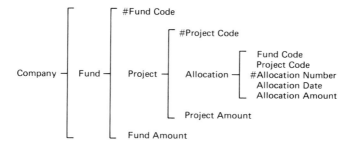

Figure 3.15   Required data structure for allocation of money.

Figure 3.16   Output data structure for employee names by employee SSN.

A situation could occur where a one-to-one relation becomes a one-to-many relation in error. For instance, a customer account may be established with an account number, with a separate account number for the same customer. The company allows only one account per customer and must notify the customer of an invalid account number.

The output data structure for a letter to a customer advising him or her of the valid and invalid account number is shown in Figure 3.19. Data sets are identified for the valid and invalid account data groups. There could be multiple invalid account groups.

The required data structure for the invalid account letters is shown in Figure 3.20. Customer Account is the primary key. The process that identifies the invalid accounts obtains both the valid and invalid account data based on the primary key and prints the letter to the customer.

Recursive entities present an interesting situation. Any employer may have one or more predecessors, i.e., several companies merged to form a new

Figure 3.17   Required data structure for employee names by employee SSN.

Figure 3.18   Required data structure for employee SSN by employee name.

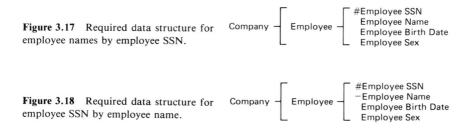

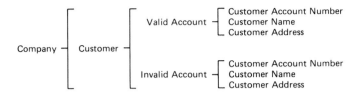

Figure 3.19   Output data structure for invalid customer accounts.

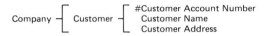

Figure 3.20   Required data structure for invalid customer accounts.

company. Each of these predecessors had the same data about his or her business that the new employer has about his or her business.

The output data structure for a list of an employer and his or her predecessors is shown in Figure 3.21. The account number, business name, and class code are shown for the new employer and for each predecessor. In addition, the transfer date and transfer percent are shown for each predecessor.

The required data structure for the employer predecessor list is shown in Figure 3.22. The predecessor entity contains only data about the transfer of the business, i.e., account number, transfer date, and transfer percent. The employer entity contains data about the employer, whether current employer or predecessor employer.

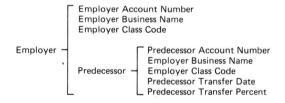

Figure 3.21   Output data structure for employer predecessors.

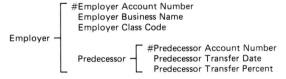

Figure 3.22   Required data structure for employer predecessors.

When there are recursive entities, the same primary key cannot be used in both entities. The primary key for employer is Employer Account Number and for predecessor is Predecessor Account Number. The Predecessor Account Number is then used to access the former employer data as Employer Account Number.

Time also presents an interesting situation. Time as a data grouping and time as a subject entity are frequently confused. For instance, Figure 3.23 shows the output data structure for a report of the weekly status of each task for each section by calendar week.

Two data sets in this structure should be changed. The Week data set within Company is really Calendar Week with a parameter for Calendar Week Date. The Week data set within Task is really a task status which is performed every week. It should be named Task Status, not Week.

The required data structure for the task status list is shown in Figure 3.24. Calendar Week has been dropped because there are no attributes required from the database. Section Number and Task Number have been identified as primary keys. Task Status needs a composite key of Task Number and Task Status Week to be unique.

Whenever time is encountered as a data set it should be reviewed carefully to determine if it is a data grouping or a subject entity. In the example below, Calendar Week is a data grouping and Task Status is a subject entity, in a many-to-one relation with Task, with a weekly frequency. Once this determination has been made, the appropriate data set name should be used.

In many instances a physical output may represent multiple logical outputs. It is the logical outputs that have data structures, not the physical output. Therefore, each output should be reviewed carefully to determine if there is one logical output or many logical outputs.

A common occurrence of multiple logical outputs is one physical report process that continually resorts the data and produces another summary. This physical report should be broken down into its logical parts and data structures composed for each logical part.

Another common occurrence is one physical screen format with multiple sequences of data. For instance, an inquiry for wages by month for an employer or by employee for an employer could use the same screen format. If

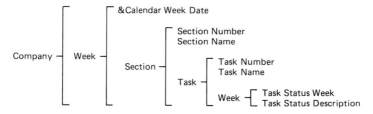

Figure 3.23 Output data structure for task status list.

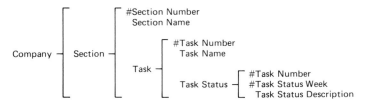

Figure 3.24 Required data structure for task status list.

search keys were entered for Employer Account Number and Month, all employees receiving wages for that month from that employer would be listed. If search keys were entered for Employer Account Number and Employee SSN, all monthly wages for that employee from that employer would be listed.

These are two separate logical outputs even though the same physical screen is used. An output data structure and a required data structure must be prepared for each logical output.

On-line systems frequently use a prompt screen for search keys. The data obtained from the database is then displayed on a second screen. The keys from these prompt screens must be added to the required data structure for the display screen. If they are not shown on the required data structure, the database may not have all the keys required.

Output data structures identify the structure of the data as it appears on the output. Required data structures show the structure of the data required from the database to support the output. Required data structures are derived from output data structures and are used to define the logical database.

If either the output data structure or the required data structure is in error, the database may well be in error. Therefore, one of the best ways to assure a good database is to prepare complete, accurate output and required data structures.

Input Data Structures

Input data structures are developed for each user input on the data flowchart. These data structures represent all data shown on the actual input. They do not have any relation to the actual storage or retrieval of data.

As each input is identified the format of the input is identified and the input data structure is developed. Like output data structures, it is not important whether the format or data structure is developed first. It is important that both are developed together.

Several symbols are used on input data structures to identify use of attributes. A left caret (◄) is used to identify an attribute that is shown on the input but is not entered into the automated system. It is not part of any automated database.

A right caret (►) is used to identify an attribute that is entered into the automated system but is not stored on the database. These attributes are generally used to verify, derive, or calculate additional attributes.

Like the output data structure, if there is no symbol prefixing an attribute, it is shown on the input, it is entered, and it is stored on the database. Occasionally, input data structures are developed where the status of an attribute is uncertain. A question mark (?) is used to indicate this uncertainty. All uncertainties must be resolved before an input data structure can become final.

Input data structures are prepared from inputs the same as output data structures are prepared from outputs. The only difference is that the data is moving into, not out of, an automated information system. Therefore, the sets of data may be different.

Outputs are based on the user needs to perform their duties, and the sets of data support those needs. Inputs are based on business events and have different sets of data. The individual attributes, however, are the same for inputs and outputs.

The individual inputs are identified on data flowcharts in the same way as outputs. Input data structures are prepared for each of these inputs the same as they are prepared for outputs. These input data structures will be used to prepare the necessary data structures.

Necessary Data Structures

Input data structures represent the structure of data shown on each input. After an input data structure is developed, a necessary data structure is prepared for that input. This necessary data structure shows the structure of the data from the input necessary to maintain the database.

A necessary data structure is developed for each input data structure. Like a required data structure, it may be developed concurrently with the input data structure, or it may be developed after the input data structure is final. Either way a necessary data structure must be developed for each input.

Several symbols are used on necessary data structures to identify the use of attributes. Primary, foreign, and secondary keys were explained in the section on entity keys and can appear on necessary data structures the same as they appear on required data structures.

A colon (:) is used to identify an attribute that is not entered but is derived, calculated, or accumulated and stored on the database. These attributes do not appear on the input data structure.

If the status of an attribute is uncertain, a question mark (?) is used, the same as on the input data structure. All uncertainties must be resolved before the necessary data structure can become final.

Necessary data structures are developed from input data structures the same as required data structures are developed from output data structures. The same procedure and rules apply, although the symbols identifying attributes may be different.

Necessary data structures will be used to verify the updating of a database. The required data structures identify what data is needed from the database. The necessary data structures show what data is needed to maintain the database. Obviously, the data maintained in the database must be the data required from the database: no more and no less.

Input and Necessary Data Structure Examples

The composition of correct input and necessary data structures is mandatory to verify that all attributes in the database are being maintained. If this verification is inaccurate or incomplete, the database may not be properly maintained. If it is not properly maintained, the best designed outputs will not produce accurate reports.

Data groupings based on business events are common on inputs. Figure 3.25 shows an input data structure for student acceptance. This acceptance data is only one portion of the total student data, but it pertains to the event of accepting a student. A data set for student acceptance is shown within the data set for student.

Student graduation data is shown on the input data structure in Figure 3.26. The graduation of a student is an event, the same as the acceptance of a student. A data set for student graduation is shown within the data set for student.

The necessary data structure for student acceptance is shown in Figure 3.27. When developing this data structure it was determined that a student could be accepted only once, giving a one-to-one relation between student and student acceptance. In this situation the attributes appear in the student data set.

If it had been determined that a student could be accepted more than once, then a one-to-many relation exists between Student and Student Acceptance. In this situation the necessary data structure would look like the input data structure in Figure 3.25 with the addition of primary keys.

The necessary data structure for student graduation is shown in Figure 3.28. Like the necessary data structure in Figure 3.27, it was determined that

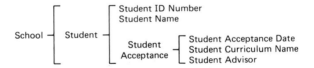

Figure 3.25 Input data structure for the student acceptance event.

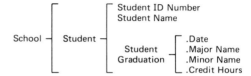

Figure 3.26 Input data structure for the student graduation event.

Figure 3.27 Necessary data structure for student acceptance.

the student could graduate only once, giving a one-to-one relation between Student and Student Graduation.

Since input and necessary data structures are used to verify maintenance of data items in the database, the structure of entities is important. In the example above it was determined from the input that a student could be accepted and could graduate only once. This placed all attributes in the student entity.

If during the development of output and required data structures it was determined that a student could be accepted and could graduate multiple times, entities would be defined for Student Acceptance and Student Graduation. Obviously, these entities would not be verified by the necessary data structures. Therefore, it is important to know the entities that are being defined.

The input data structure for a license application is shown in Figure 3.29. Applicant Weight is entered but it will not be stored on the database. Applicant Signature appears on the application form but is not entered into the automated system.

The necessary data structure for the license application is shown in Figure 3.30. Applicant Number has been added as a computer-generated field,

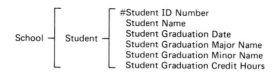

Figure 3.28 Necessary data structure for student graduation.

Figure 3.29 Input data structure for license application.

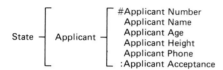

Figure 3.30 Necessary data structure for license application.

and it has been identified as the primary key. Applicant Acceptance has been added as a derived field. Both Applicant Weight and Applicant Signature have been dropped.

Menus and Prompts

In today's on-line environment the use of menu screens and prompt screens is common. Menus are usually lists of functions that can be selected and do not involve the database. For this reason data structures are not used for database design. They are used, however, for developing the menu program.

Prompts are screens that request certain key data to access the database. Even though these are input screens they really pertain to outputs. The keys requested on prompt screens must be used to identify primary and secondary keys on required data structures.

The actual display of prompts and menu screens is an output. If data structures were prepared for these screens, they should be output data structures. Usually, no required data structures are needed because no data is required from the database.

Input/Output Screens

On-line updating is also common in today's environment. An update screen is really two logical screens: one for output and one for input. An output and a required data structure must be prepared for the output function of the screen. An input and a necessary data structure must be prepared for the input function of the screen.

In some situations these two sets of data structures are the same. However, in many situations the two sets of data structures are different. To avoid any assumptions, and resulting discrepancies in the database, both sets of data structures must be prepared.

Necessary data structures are also developed for any other internal updates to the database that do not have input formats or input data structures. These internal updates must be identified to assure that internal databases are properly defined.

Input data structures identify the structure of data as it enters the system. Necessary data structures show the structure of data necessary to maintain the database. Necessary data structures are derived from input data structures and are used to verify the design of the logical database.

If either the input data structure or necessary data structure is in error, the database could be in error. Errors in the logical database design derived from output data structures may well go undetected. Therefore, one of the best ways to assure a good database is to prepare good, accurate input and necessary data structures.

DATA STRUCTURE DECOMPOSITION

The required data structures are used to define the output logical database. The necessary data structures are used to verify that all attributes on the output logical database are maintained and there are no unnecessary attributes. This is the principle behind data-structured database design.

The required and necessary data structures must be decomposed before they can be used to define or verify the logical database. Data structure decomposition is the process of breaking a data structure apart by entity, aggregating attributes within each entity, and maintaining the data relations and access paths between entities. These entities, data relations, and their access paths form the logical database.

The method of decomposing a data structure is the same for both required and necessary data structures. Each data set in the data structure should be an entity and all attributes should be in the database. All data groupings, parameters, literals, and calculated attributes should have been removed.

Entity Separation

The first step in decomposing a data structure is to separate each data set in the structure from its parent data set. This process begins at the right, or lowest-level entity, of a data structure and proceeds to the left. Since each data set is an entity, it is really entities that are being decoupled.

Before each data set is separated from its parent, the identity of the parent entity is kept as a foreign key in the subordinate entity. This foreign key is the primary key of the parent entity stored in the subordinate entity to show which parent entity occurrence owns the subordinate entity occurrence. When parent entity attributes are needed, the foreign key is used to obtain the parent occurrence.

However, this foreign key is needed only if there is a requirement to access the parent entity from the subordinate entity. On the other hand, if there is no need to access the parent entity from the subordinate entity, there is no need for a foreign key. Foreign keys are needed only when there is access up the data structure.

If the access is down the data structure, the subordinate entity needs to contain a secondary key. This secondary key is the primary key of the parent entity stored in the subordinate entity for access into that entity. If there is no access from the parent entity to the subordinate entity, there is no need for the secondary key.

Any subordinate entity must have either a foreign key or a secondary key to identify the parent entity. The attribute is the same in either case, i.e., the primary key of the parent. It is identified either as a foreign key or a secondary key based on the direction of access.

The direction of access must be determined before a data structure is decomposed. It could be determined as the data structure is being composed or just before it is decomposed. Either way is acceptable as long as the direction of access is determined before decomposition.

To determine the direction of access, the data structure is reviewed to determine which entity actually drives the data structure. The entity that is accessed first is the entity that drives the data structure. Access to other entities in the data structure will be made from this driver entity.

For instance, there are many wages for an employee and the wages are being processed randomly. Employee data is needed for each wage being processed, so access is up the data structure from Wage to Employee. Wage is the driver entity, and a foreign key for Employee SSN is included in the Wage entity as shown in Figure 3.31.

If, however, a report is prepared for all wages for an employee and employees are processed in SSN order, Employee is the driver entity. All wage data is needed for each Employee, so access is down the data structure. A secondary key for Employee SSN is included in the Wage entity, as shown in Figure 3.32.

The addition of a foreign or secondary key to the Wage entity creates data redundancy. Employee SSN appears in both the employee entity and the wage entity. This redundancy is necessary to provide access between wage and employee. Data-structured database design does not eliminate redundancy, but it limits it to access keys.

Earlier it was emphasized that primary keys must be unique or they are not true primary keys. It should be obvious that if a designated primary key were not unique, i.e., there were multiple employees for the same SSN, the foreign key would be meaningless. It would be impossible to determine to

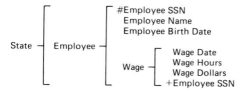

Figure 3.31 Foreign key for access up the data structure.

Figure 3.32 Secondary key for access down the data structure.

which employee a wage belonged. To prevent this situation, primary keys must be unique.

Uniqueness must be explained further. Assume that each employee has only one SSN and that each SSN is assigned to only one employee. One occurrence of employee information for each employee would be uniquely identified by a primary key of Employee SSN.

If, for whatever reasons, there were multiple occurrences for an employee, the Employee SSN would uniquely identify the employee, but not each specific occurrence for that employee. Employee SSN would be considered a primary key with respect to employee, but not with respect to occurrences for that employee. Another attribute would need to be added to form a compound key to identify uniquely each occurrence for the employee.

If, for whatever reasons, two employees had the same SSN, Employee SSN could not be considered a primary key. Additional attributes would need to be identified as a compound key to identify each employee uniquely.

In the general course of business, errors do occur. If Employee SSN were used as a primary key and it was entered in error such that two employees have the same apparent SSN, the primary key is not invalid. The intent is that Employee SSN is the primary key.

In this situation Employee SSN could be used to obtain all occurrences matching that SSN so that a correction could be made. In other words, a primary key can be used to prevent errors from entering the database, or to identify errors before they have been entered.

When decomposing required data structures, the equal sign (=) used to identify supportive attributes is dropped. It serves no purpose in the logical database. Its only use was to identify attributes on required data structures that supported outputs but were not actually output themselves.

The colon (:) used to identify derived attributes on necessary data structures is also dropped. It serves no purpose in the logical database. Its only use was to identify attributes on necessary data structures that were derived, calculated, or accumulated and did not appear on the input themselves.

Any questionable attributes (?) must be resolved before the decomposition can be complete. They are used on necessary and required data structures to identify attributes that are questionable. If they are questionable before decomposition, they are certainly questionable after decomposition and must be resolved.

The keys needed to access an entity are also documented during decomposition. Different access paths may require different groups of keys. All of these key groups must be known when the physical database is developed or the required access paths may not be available.

For instance, employers might normally be accessed by Employer Account Number, which is the primary key for Employer. But there could be a data structure showing access to Employer by Employer Class Code and Employer Establishment Date, and another data structure for access by Employer Business Type Code. All three of these accesses must be documented when decomposing data structures.

The sequence of attributes in a key group is important. The sequence designates the order in which data will be obtained from the database. Changing the sequence of attributes in a key group will change the order in which data will be obtained from the database.

The access path in each data structure must be reviewed carefully to determine the sequence of attributes in a key group. After decomposition of all the data structures, the total collection of key groups for an entity will be known. These groups can be reviewed and if adjustments are necessary, the data structures can be modified.

In some instances an access path into an entity will not include the primary key, yet a primary key must be designated because there are subordinate entities. In this situation an asterisk (*) is used to designate the primary key that is not used in that access. When the key groups are listed during decomposition, primary keys identified with an asterisk are not included.

During decomposition the data relations between entities are documented. All subordinate entities are listed for each parent entity. This list of subordinates is used to develop a data relation chart and identify many-to-many data relations.

Data structure separation is an important process. It provides the entities, attributes, primary keys, data relations, and data accesses needed to define the logical database. This information is eventually used to develop the physical database.

Attribute Aggregation

The second step in data structure decomposition is to logically add all attributes, data relations, and access key groups for each entity. This logical addition provides a complete view of the total requirements for each entity in the database as derived from the individual data structures. This complete view includes the entities, their primary keys, their attributes, their access paths, and the data relations between entities.

Attributes are logically added by entity for each entity on the data structure. For instance, two data structures containing the Employee entity are decomposed, giving the two sets of Employee attributes shown in Figure 3.33.

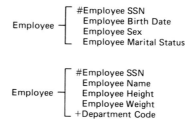

Figure 3.33 Two additional sets of decomposed employee data.

Employee SSN is the primary key used for access in both sets and Department Code is a foreign key in one set.

The result of the logical addition of these sets of employee data is shown in Figure 3.34. If these are the only data structures involved in decomposition, this is the logical database for the employee entity. If other data structures are involved, more attributes might be added to the employee logical database.

Key groups are logically added for each entity in a similar manner. The three access paths for employer mentioned earlier result in the three key groups shown in Figure 3.35. The first group is the primary key for normal access and the other two groups contain secondary keys.

Data relations are also logically added for each entity. Subordinates are combined for each parent entity, giving a complete list of all parent entities and the subordinates for each parent. This list is used to develop a chart of data relations in the database, and to identify and resolve any many-to-many relations.

For instance, separation and aggregation of several data structures might result in the data relations shown in Figure 3.36. It should be obvious from these data relations that Wage has two parents: Employee and Position. It should also be apparent that Employee and Position are in a many-to-many relation that must be resolved.

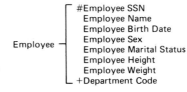

Figure 3.34 Logical addition of employee attributes.

Figure 3.35 Multiple key groups for employer entity.

Company
   Employee
   Position

Employee
   Wage
   Position

Position
   Employee   **Figure 3.36**   Data relations after separa-
   Wage   tion and aggregation of data structures.

Many-to-Many Relations

If a many-to-many relation exists between two entities, foreign and secondary keys are useless. For instance, employers can have many employees, and employees can have many employers. Figure 3.37 shows two data structures for listing employers by employee and employees by employer.

The results of decomposition of these two data structures are shown in Figure 3.38. Each entity contains a foreign key to the other entity. This may seem reasonable, but when there are multiple parent occurrences, what value is contained in the foreign key? If an employee worked for three employers, which Employer Account Number is carried as the foreign key? Is each account number carried as a foreign key?

The answer is that foreign and secondary keys cannot be used for entities with a many-to-many relation. Another entity must be used to resolve the many-to-many relation with two one-to-many relations. That new entity must be a child to both entities involved in the many-to-many relation.

Wages are a transaction between employer and employee. There is a one-

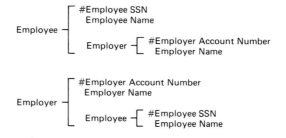

Figure 3.37   Entities with a many-to-many relation.

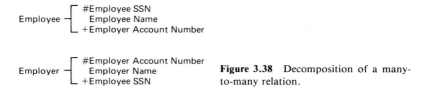

Figure 3.38   Decomposition of a many-to-many relation.

to-many relation between employer and wages, and between employee and wages. Each wage has only one employer and one employee. Wage would carry a foreign key to both employer and employee.

However, the primary key for wage must be identified before foreign keys are added. To identify each wage uniquely, a composite key of Wage Date, Employer Account Number, and Employee SSN is needed. Figure 3.39 shows the wage data structure.

Since Employer Account Number and Employee SSN already exist as a composite key in the wage entity, they are not added as a foreign key. They can still be used to access Employee and Employer, but they are not identified as a foreign key.

Compound and Composite Keys

When a parent entity contains a compound or composite key, all attributes of that key are used in the child entity as a foreign or secondary key. Figure 3.40 shows a data structure for citations issued to drivers. Driver has a compound key of Driver Name and Driver Birth Date which is inserted as a compound foreign key in Citation before decomposition.

Multiple Foreign Keys

The examples above showed only one foreign key for an entity. If an entity is subordinate to several parent entities, a foreign key is needed for each parent entity. These foreign keys are needed to provide access to each parent entity.

The data structure for legal documents by employer they are issued to, and the data structure for legal documents by the issuing court, are shown in Figure 3.41. In this situation a document has two parents: Employer, with a primary key of Employer Account Number, and issuing Court, with a primary key of Court ID. The primary key for a document is Document Number.

```
                             ┌─ #Employer Account Number
                             │  #Employee SSN
                    Wage ─┤  #Wage Date
                             │  Wage Hours
                             │  Wage Type
                             └─ Wage Dollars
```

Figure 3.39 Wage data structure.

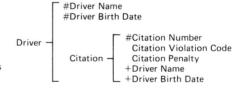

Figure 3.40 Data structure for citations issued to drivers.

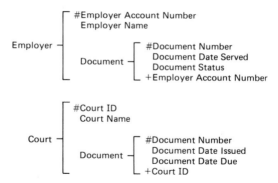

Figure 3.41   Document entity with multiple parents.

Decomposition of these two data structures yields the document data structure shown in Figure 3.42. All the attributes for a document have been logically aggregated, showing foreign keys for both Employer and Court.

Priority of Keys

The identification of keys within an entity follows a priority scheme. Primary, composite, and compound keys have the highest priority. Secondary keys have the next priority, and foreign keys have the lowest priority.

Primary keys have the highest priority because they uniquely identify each occurrence in an entity and provide access to that entity. Secondary keys are less important because they only provide access to an entity. Foreign keys are least important because they are used only to leave that entity and access another entity.

Therefore, an attribute identified as a primary key cannot be reduced to a secondary or a foreign key. Similarly, a secondary key cannot be reduced to a foreign key. In other words, if an attribute already exists in an entity as a primary or secondary key, it is not identified as a foreign key. If the attribute already exists but not as a primary or secondary key, it can be identified as a foreign key.

Data structure decomposition is an important step in the process of defining databases. It separates the subject entities from individual data struc-

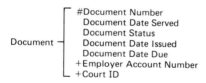

Figure 3.42 Decomposition and aggregation of document entity with multiple parents.

tures and aggregates the attributes by entity. It also identifies the data relations and access paths between entities.

When the logical database has been identified by the data structure decomposition process, the physical database can be developed. Criteria for developing the physical database are explained briefly in Chapter 5.

The data structure decomposition process also provides the information to develop a data entity model. This model is useful for developing the physical database and for developing a deep understanding of the organization and structure of the company's data.

SUMMARY

The composition and decomposition of data structures is a formal process. Data structures are composed to represent the inputs and outputs of a system and their database requirements. The required and necessary data structures are then decomposed and the attributes and access paths are aggregated to form subject databases.

These subject databases are then accessed by the applications. This method establishes data independence so that the data is not bound directly to an application. Data is managed by subject, and subsets of data are manipulated by specific applications.

The independence of applications and subject data allows each to be more flexible in today's dynamic business environment. Sets of data and sets of process logic are manipulated to meet the changing business needs of a company. The result is not only increased productivity, but an increased chance for company survival.

STUDY QUESTIONS

1. What is the difference between output and required data structures?
2. How are required and necessary data structures similar?
3. What symbols are used to identify the use of attributes?
4. What is a transaction entity?
5. What is a single-occurrence entity?
6. What data structures are prepared for update screens?
7. What is a data grouping?
8. How are data structures composed?
9. How are data structures decomposed?
10. How is data independence established?

4

DESIGN MODELS

A model is a preliminary representation of the arrangement and relationship of elements in a system. It is a prototype of a system to be refined and improved. It is the original pattern for building a system.

A model is also a plan for constructing a new system or for modifying an existing system. After the system is built the model becomes documentation about the system. It is a graphic explanation of a system.

A system is any set of related elements combined to form a whole and operate in unison. It is a set of facts, principles, and rules, arranged in an orderly fashion. It is a logical plan linking all the elements.

The systems described here are information systems. The elements of these information systems are processes and data. These elements are the basic, essential components of information systems.

A process is a particular method of doing something. It involves a number of steps or operations to achieve an end result. The processes in information systems are data manipulation processes.

Data are the individual facts and figures that are manipulated, stored, and retrieved. They are the basic components of information from which conclusions can be drawn. They collectively provide information from which decisions are made.

Information systems can support business activities, scientific inquiry, manufacturing processes, etc. They have a wide range of uses that is expanding daily. However, information systems as described here pertain largely to business activities within a company.

A company is any business enterprise, corporation, partnership, governmental agency, industrial firm, or other group of people organized for a common goal. These companies perform a variety of business activities to achieve that goal. Each of these activities consists of processes and data.

Four different design models are used to represent the activities, processes, and data in a company. These models form the meta-model representing the company and the information it needs to do business. Each of these models has a definite purpose and use in the design and documentation of information systems.

The benefits of these design models range from a graphic view (a picture is worth a thousand words) to investigation of "what if" alternatives. They are used for both planning and documentation. Without them, the chances for a truly successful system are minimal.

BUSINESS ENTITY MODEL

Any company performs a variety of business activities. During the performance of these activities the company deals with a variety of business entities. These business entities may be within the company or outside the company.

Business Entity Definitions

An entity can be a being, such as a person, creature, or organism; a thing, such as an object, article, or item; or a unit, such as a division, section, or team. In terms of a company's business activities an entity is a person, a group of people, a place, or a thing.

A business entity is any discrete, definable unit with which a company interacts while performing its business activities. That unit may be another company, a governmental agency, an organizational unit within a company or governmental agency, or a person. Simply stated, a business entity is a person or an organizational unit.

A business transaction is any transaction that occurs between business entities. That transaction can occur between different people, between different organizational entities, or between people and organizational units. It is a transactional entity that flows between business entities.

A business entity model is a representation of the architecture of the business world from the company's perspective. It shows the business entities, both inside and outside the company, and the business transactions between those entities. It is a model of who the company deals with and the transactions with them.

Two symbols are used to construct a business entity model. A hexagon designates a business entity, with the name of that entity placed inside the hexagon. Figure 4.1 shows a business entity for Employee.

Figure 4.1 Symbol for a business entity.

An arrow designates a business transaction between business entities. The name of the transaction is placed on the arrow. Figure 4.2 shows a wage transaction between the employer and employee business entities.

Business Entity Model Rules

A business entity model is developed using only these two symbols. The model is relatively easy to develop if a few simple rules are followed.

A business transaction must occur between two business entities; i.e., it must leave a hexagon and go to a hexagon. It cannot go to a business entity without a source and it cannot leave a business entity with no destination. Figure 4.3 shows two business transactions that are incorrect.

Business entity names must be unique within the company. Two or more business entities cannot have the same name. If there are identical names, there are either redundant business entities or invalid business entity names. Either situation must be corrected.

Business transaction names must be unique to a specific transaction. Any unique business transaction must have its own name. That transaction, however, can appear more than once on a business entity model. This situation occurs when the same transaction is sent to more than one business entity.

A business entity cannot be shown without any connecting transactions. This situation indicates that the company has no information exchange with that business entity. If there is no information exchange, the business entity does not need to be on the business entity model. If there is information exchange, the transaction must be identified and placed on the model.

A business transaction cannot flow in two directions. It can only flow from one business entity to another business entity. If that transaction is modified and returned to the originating business entity, it should have a different name.

Business transactions cannot diverge or converge between business entities. Each business transaction must flow directly from one business entity

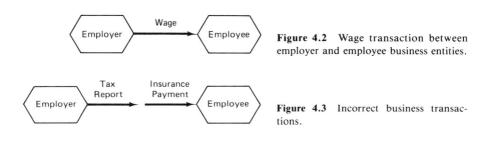

Figure 4.2 Wage transaction between employer and employee business entities.

Figure 4.3 Incorrect business transactions.

to another business entity. If business transactions do actually converge or diverge, they must occur in a business entity, not between business entities.

If there are multiple business transactions, each must be shown on a separate arrow. If a business transaction has multiple parts but flows as a unit and is named as a unit, it may be shown as one transaction.

If too many transactions are flowing to or from a business entity, that entity should probably be subdivided into several smaller business entities. This situation occurs when one business entity symbol is drawn for an entire company. A separate business entity should be identified for each unit within the company.

Business Entity Model Development

A typical business entity model is shown in Figure 4.4. The business entities are employer, employee, court, agency, and claimant. Seven different business transactions flow between these five business entities. Employers pay wages to employees. Claimants file claims to, and receive benefit payments from, the agency. The employer makes tax payments to, and receives benefit charges from, the government agency. Employers file insolvencies and the agency files disputes with the court.

Business entity models are used to understand the business world and how the company fits into that world. They are also used for planning the development of information systems. A thorough understanding of the business world, and the information needed for a company to survive in that world, is a distinct advantage when designing information systems.

Business entity models also identify data entities that will be used in developing information systems. Each business entity and each business transaction is a separate data entity. Correct identification of business entities and business transactions is the first step in correct data definition.

In the example shown in Figure 4.4 there are 12 data entities: employer, employee, court, agency, claimant, insolvency, wage, dispute, benefit charge,

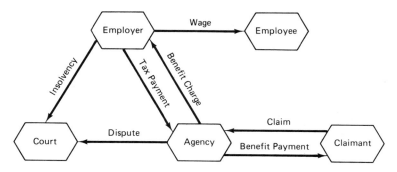

Figure 4.4 Typical business entity model.

tax payment, claim, and benefit payment. Each of these data entities will contain attributes that describe the entity.

The input for a business entity model is obtained from a description of the business environment. This description may be obtained in a number of ways. Usually, most of the business entities and transactions are identified early in the design from user descriptions. However, refinements can be made through the design process.

Business entity models must be developed in the early stages of system design. They cannot be developed before system design because they will not benefit from the problem analysis aspect of system design. They cannot be developed after system design because the data entities may not be correctly defined. Therefore, business entity models must be developed concurrent with system design.

Multiple business entity models may be prepared for planning purposes. When business alternatives are being discussed, a business entity model can be most useful for discussing each alternative and comparing alternatives.

When a company decides to develop a business entity model, the entire model is usually not developed at one time. The model is usually started as a prototype, then refined and expanded over a period of time. This approach produces a better model than does a short-term, all-out effort.

If an entire business entity model is to be developed at one time, it should be a well-planned project. That project should have a firm commitment to produce a correct, complete model. If not, the model will be useless and may actually be detrimental for developing information systems.

The starting point for a prototype business entity model is the next new information system or major upgrade to an existing information system. As each new system or system upgrade is encountered, the model is expanded to include that system. Refinements are made to the model as each system is being enhanced.

When business entity models are developed, the entire business must be included. A common mistake is to include only the business entities and transactions that occur in automated information systems. This is an extremely nearsighted approach that will eventually be to the detriment of the company.

The objective is to build a model to understand how the company operates and then build information systems to assist that operation. If the model is incomplete, it is impossible to understand how the company operates since only a limited part of the operation is shown. If the total company operation is not understood, successful information systems cannot be developed.

Any company needs information to operate successfully. That information may be automated or manually processed, but it is still needed to operate successfully. The business entity model must include all business entities and business transactions to provide the best base possible for survival.

Another common mistake is to allow a business entity model to evolve into a data flowchart. Any time that a business entity model begins to look

Figure 4.5 Invalid business entity.

like a data flowchart the development process must stop and the model must be corrected. The different symbols for business entity models and data flowcharts will help identify this situation.

A business entity is a person or group of people. It is an entity that can take action on a business transaction. If a business entity is defined that cannot take action on a transaction, it must be removed.

An example of a nonaction business entity is shown in Figure 4.5. A student may register for a class; however, the student registers with the registrar. The registrar takes action on the registration. The class cannot take action on the registration; therefore, it cannot be a business entity.

Occasionally, a business entity model is used to show the relations between data entities. This is not the function of a business entity model. Data relations are shown on the data entity model described later.

A business entity model shows only the business entities a company deals with and the transactions between those entities. The business entities are people or organizational units that take action on business transactions. The model's purpose is to understand the business environment and to identify data entities. Any other use defeats the value of the model.

BUSINESS INFORMATION MODEL

Each company performs a variety of business activities to meet its goals. These business activities include physical processes and informational processes, both of which need data to function properly. If the flow of data between these processes is incomplete, the processes cannot be performed properly.

A model can be developed for either physical or informational processes. A physical process model shows physical processes, physical resources flowing between processes, and the storages needed to supply resources to the processes. The processes may be either assembly or disassembly, with one or more supplies being used and one or more items being produced.

Physical Process Model

The same symbols are used in a process model as are used in data flowcharts. A rectangle represents a process with the name of the process inside the rectangle. A storage is indicated by a "box with bulging sides" with the name of the storage inside. A data flow is represented by an arrow with the name of the data flow on the arrow.

Figure 4.6 Physical process model for assembling an automobile.

A physical process model for assembling an automobile is shown in Figure 4.6. Although it is a small example, it shows the materials going into each process and a product coming out of each process. It is a typical example of a manufacturing process.

A physical model for disassembling a cow, commonly known as slaughtering, is shown in Figure 4.7. It is similar to the assembly model above except that there are multiple products coming out of a process rather than just one product. A process model must be able to show processes with multiple inputs and multiple outputs.

Information Model

An information process model shows information processes, data flowing between processes, and the storages needed to hold data for future use. Like the physical processes, the information processes may have multiple inputs and multiple outputs. Figure 4.8 shows an information process model for approving payment of claims. All claims received are reviewed and either rejected or approved. All approved claims are paid based on type of claim and client history.

This example is typical of information processes with multiple inputs and multiple outputs. The Claim Review process has one input and two outputs. The Claim Payment process has two inputs and one output.

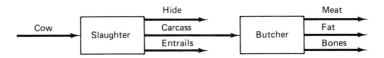

Figure 4.7 Physical process model for slaughtering a cow.

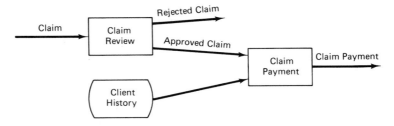

Figure 4.8 Information process model for payment of claims.

The physical process model and the information process model differ only in what is flowing between the processes. In the physical model materials flow between processes, and in the information model data flows between processes. Since data is a resource that is managed the same as any other business resource, there is no basic difference between the two models.

Therefore, a process model can be developed for any set of processes, the resources flowing between those processes and resource storages. For the purpose of designing business applications and databases, the process model represents business information processes, the data flowing between those processes, and data storages. Therefore, the term *business information model* is used.

The business information model represents the highest-level architecture of business processes, data flows, and data storages. It is used to examine the company's business, to understand how it operates, and to plan its information management. It sets the base for strategic and tactical planning of information processes and databases.

To be fully effective, the model must include all information systems in the business, not just those that have been automated. It must include the total system, whether manual or automated. In other words, all information systems in the company must be shown on the business information model.

The business information model is similar to a data flowchart. However, it is a level higher than the system data flowchart, and includes all systems in the business. It shows all the major business processes, data flows, and data storages in the business.

Business Information Model Development

There are two ways to develop a business information model. The first is functional decomposition, where the business is decomposed into its basic functions, activities, and tasks, with the data flowing between them. The second is system combination, where the existing information systems are combined to describe the business functions.

In actual practice both methods are used to build the initial business information model. Each method provides a different view of the business processes, the data flows, and how each process uses the data. The logical combination of these two methods provides the prototype business information model that is continuously refined to represent the business.

Functional decomposition of the business begins with the company represented as one process, with the major flows into and out of that business. This business process is then decomposed into its major business functions, such as manufacturing, research, sales, personnel, etc., with the data flowing between these functions. Each of these business functions is decomposed into major activities with the data flowing between them.

A typical business with the major data flows into and out of that business

Figure 4.9 Top level business information model.

is shown in Figure 4.9. Most businesses will have many inputs and many outputs. These inputs and outputs can be grouped by function and shown with fewer data flows. The company is decomposed into its major functions, including the data flows between those functions, as shown in Figure 4.10.

In this simple example the company consists of manufacturing, personnel, and fiscal. In actual practice there may be many more functional areas and many more data flows.

During functional decomposition the data flows must match between parent and child. The processes and data flows must be specifically and uniquely named. Major data storages must be shown and must also be specifically and uniquely named. The rules used for data flowcharts apply to business information models.

Decomposition ends when the processes become major tasks. Although it is difficult to state exactly how many levels of decomposition occur, it is apparent when a business process becomes a major task. The model produced by this process is the functionally decomposed business information model.

System combination begins by taking the highest-level data flowcharts from each information system in the company and combining them. Common data flows are connected to join the systems together. In many instances the data flow names must be analyzed to determine if they are common. The model produced by this process is the system combination business information model.

Data storages are also used to combine system-level data flowcharts. Even if there are no data flows between major systems, they may share the same data storages. These shared data storages are used to connect the systems.

The combination of several information systems into a business model is shown in Figure 4.11. The License Issuance process receives applications and issues licenses. The Citation Tracking process receives citations and main-

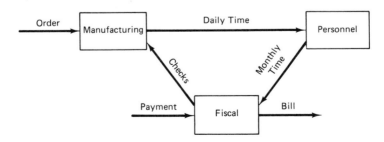

Figure 4.10 Functionally decomposed business information model.

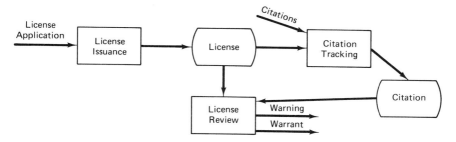

Figure 4.11 System combination business information model.

tains a citation storage. The License Review process reviews the citation storage and the license storage and issues warnings and warrants.

The functionally decomposed model and the system combination model are logically combined to form a prototype business information model. If the existing information systems were developed to meet the business needs, the system combination model will closely match the functional decomposition model. If the existing information systems were developed in a haphazard, unplanned manner that did not meet the business needs, the two models would be far from agreement.

In situations where the system combination model is far from agreement with the functional decomposition model, both models must be maintained. The system combination model is maintained to represent the information systems as they exist. The functional decomposition model is maintained to represent the business environment and how information systems should be developed.

When combining the functional decomposition model and the system combination model, the question arises as to whether the company should be organized around its information, or whether the information should be organized around the company. Basically, the information systems should be organized around the business functions. However, the organization of information systems may indicate possible reorganization of the business functions.

This question is not quite as important with the concept of company-wide databases. The information systems can meet the need of the business functions regardless of how those functions are organized. The databases are organized by subject and can meet the needs of any information system or business function.

Once a prototype business information model is developed, it is maintained as the model of the business. It can also be modified to represent a predicted business environment. Information systems must be developed or enhanced according to this business information model.

As the business information model gets larger, it is difficult to place the storages and processes in convenient positions so that storages are close to processes and there are a minimum of data flows crossing. When this situation occurs, multiple data storage symbols are used to represent the same data storage and they are placed close to the processes that use them. The flow of data between processes is of primary importance and the location of data storages is of secondary importance.

Manufacturing processes require business information the same as do managerial business processes. Manufacturing processes are also shown on a business information model, with the data flowing into and out of those processes. The supplies and products of the manufacturing process are not shown.

Over a period of time, and with careful planning, the system combination model will match the functional decomposition model. When this happens, information systems will truly support the business. Until it happens, there must be very careful planning and prioritization to assure that information systems are developed or enhanced to meet company needs.

DATA ENTITY MODEL

In a formal database environment, data is stored by subject entity. All the data about one subject is stored in one subject data file. The business processes access the subject data files to obtain data needed for outputs or to update data obtained from inputs.

A data entity is a single subject of data, i.e., a customer. Each data entity contains one or more attributes of data that describe that entity. Collectively, these data entities and their attributes form the company's database.

Data entities are identified from two sources. First, all business entities and all business transactions from the business entity model are data entities. In addition, data entities are identified on the necessary and required data structures. Whether they are identified on the business entity model, on data structures, or both, these are the only two sources for identifying data entities.

A data entity model shows the logical architecture of the company's database. It shows all the data entities, the relations between the entities, the access paths between the entities, and the structure of the attributes in each entity. It does not show the flow of data between data entities.

One data entity model is created for the entire company's database. It shows all data entities regardless of their physical repository, format, or size. It is modified as the database changes.

The data entity model contains three submodels. The logical data relation submodel shows the data entities and the relations between entities. The logical data structure submodel shows the data attributes and primary keys for each entity. The logical data access submodel shows the data attributes and access keys for each access path.

Logical Data Relations

The logical data relation submodel shows each data entity in the database and the data relations between each entity. Two symbols are used to develop a logical data relation chart. A "box with bulging sides" designates a data entity with the name of the entity written inside the box, as shown in Figure 4.12.

A dashed line with an arrow designates a data relation between data entities. The arrow points from the parent entity to the subordinate entity. The line is dashed to indicate that it is a relation, not a data flow. A logical data relation chart does not show data flows.

The data relation between Claimant and Insurance Claim is shown in Figure 4.13. Each claimant can have many insurance claims. Therefore, the arrow points from Claimant to Insurance Claim.

An arrow pointing in one direction indicates a one-to-many data relation between entities. Each occurrence of the parent entity has, or can have, many occurrences in the subordinate entity. The arrow points from the one occurrence to the many occurrences.

An arrow pointing in both directions indicates a many-to-many data relation between entities. Each occurrence of the first entity has many occurrences in the second entity, and each occurrence of the second entity has many occurrences in the first entity.

A many-to-many data relation is shown in Figure 4.14. Each employer can have many employees, and each employee can work for many employers. The arrow between Employer and Employee points in both directions.

During database design many-to-many data relations need to be resolved to one-to-many relations with a common data entity. This resolution is shown by a single arrow from each data entity involved in the many-to-many relation to the common data entity. This common data entity is referred to as a transaction entity.

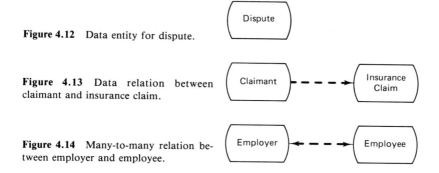

Figure 4.12   Data entity for dispute.

Figure 4.13   Data relation between claimant and insurance claim.

Figure 4.14   Many-to-many relation between employer and employee.

The addition of a wage data entity to resolve the many-to-many relation between Employer and Employee is shown in Figure 4.15. Wage is the transaction between Employer and Employee and is therefore common to both Employer and Employee.

Each employer pays many wages, and each employee receives many wages. However, any individual wage belongs to only one employer and only one employee. Therefore, Wage is the entity that resolves the many-to-many relation between Employer and Employee.

Access paths are the routes for navigating between entities in a database. The access paths are indicated by the data relations on the data entity chart.

Each one-to-many data relation is an access path. Access in the direction of the arrow, i.e., from the one occurrence to the many occurrences, is an access path to a subordinate entity to obtain all occurrences of that entity using the primary key of the parent. Access against the direction of the arrow, i.e., from the many occurrences to the one occurrence, is an access to the parent entity using a foreign key in the subordinate entity.

The many-to-many relations are not access paths. Neither entity is the parent entity, or the subordinate entity, or conversely each entity is both a parent entity and a subordinate entity. Therefore, neither entity can contain foreign keys to the other entity and there can be no access path between them.

Logical data relations are developed from the decomposition of data structures. The decomposition process produces the data entities and identifies data relations. Based on this information the logical data relation chart can be drawn.

Each date entity is drawn as a "bulging box." The one-to-many relations are shown with dashed arrows. When a one-to-many relation occurs both ways between two data entities, a many-to-many relation exists.

Relatiuns cannot converge or diverge between data entities. Each arrow must go from one data entity to another data entity. An arrow cannot leave a data entity with no destination or appear to originate from nowhere and go to a data entity.

A data entity can exist by itself. It does not have to have relations with or access paths to or from any other data entities.

The data relations defined by data structure decomposition show only the data relations and access paths defined by the user requirements. Other

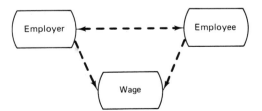

Figure 4.15 Wage transaction entity.

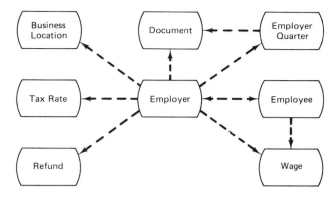

Figure 4.16 Typical data entity chart.

data relations and access paths may exist, but will be identified as they are defined.

A typical data entity chart is shown in Figure 4.16. A variety of data entities, data relations, and access paths are shown.

Logical Data Structure

The logical data structure submodel shows the data structure of a logical database. It shows the data entities in the database and the data attributes and keys in each entity. It shows the contents of each data entity in the database, but not the data relations or access paths between entities.

A brief data entity structure is shown in Figure 4.17. It shows a portion

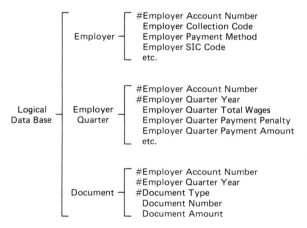

Figure 4.17 Typical data entity structure.

of the attributes in the entities shown in Figure 4.16. The primary, secondary, and foreign keys are also identified.

A logical data structure is developed from the decomposition of necessary and required data structures. The data sets are separated and the attributes and keys are aggregated by subject entity to form a complete list of all attributes in each entity.

Logical Data Accesses

The logical data access submodel shows the keys required to navigate between entities in the database. They are the keys required to move along an access path and access an entity. They are the entry points into an entity.

Logical data accesses contain groups of keys, with each group containing one or more primary or secondary key attributes. These attributes are listed in the order the data is to be stored or retrieved. A typical list of data accesses for wages is shown in Figure 4.18.

The logical data accesses are obtained from the decomposition of necessary and required data structures. As each entity is decoupled the primary and secondary keys in that entity are recorded as a key group which represents the access to that entity for that data structure. When the decomposition of all data structures is completed, all key groups will be identified for each entity.

The data entity model consists of three submodels: logical data relations, logical data structure, and logical data accesses. This model represents the logical database as defined by the user requirements. It is used both as documentation of the logical database and to design the physical database.

Logical data relations show the data entities and the relations between data entities. They do not show the attributes in each entity or the keys used for access.

The logical data structure shows the data entities and the attributes and keys in each entity. It supplements the data entity chart with attributes and keys for navigating between entities.

Logical data accesses show the key groups that are used to access each entity. They are the entry points into an entity to obtain occurrences based on the value of the keys.

#Employer Account Number
#Employee SSN
#Wage Quarter

#Employee SSN
−Wage Type

#Employee SSN
#Employer Account Number
−Wage Type

Figure 4.18 Logical data accesses for wages.

The data entity model is developed from the required and necessary data structures. It must be kept current with each change on those data structures. If it is not kept current, the chances for a successful database are minimal.

DATABASE MODEL

A formal database environment includes both a logical database design and a physical database design. The logical database design must be done first based on the user requirements. It cannot be influenced or constrained in any way by the physical environment.

Once the logical database design is completed, the physical database design can begin. The physical design process adapts the logical design to a specific physical operating environment. It does not change the logical design, it only adapts it to the physical environment.

The logical database design is represented by the data entity model. That model shows the entities, attributes, and keys that comprise the logical database. These are the building blocks for the physical database.

The physical database consists of physical files, records, and data items. The physical files represent the logical data entities. The physical records represent logical occurrences of an entity. The data items represent the logical attributes in an entity.

The database model is a representation of the physical database. It shows the physical files, the access paths between the files, and the data items in each file. It is similar to the data entity model, but for the physical database.

The database model consists of two submodels. The physical data access submodel shows the physical files and the access paths between files. The physical data structure submodel shows the structure of the files and data items in each file.

Physical Data Accesses

The physical data access chart shows each physical file in the database and the access paths between those files. Two symbols are used to develop a database chart. An oval indicates a physical file with the name of the file written inside the oval as shown in Figure 4.19.

A dashed line with an arrow designates an access path between physical files. The arrow points from the file with one occurrence to the file with many occurrences, the same as on the data entity chart. The line is dashed to indicate that it is an access path, not a data flow.

Figure 4.19 Symbol for physical file.

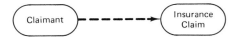

Figure 4.20 Physical access path between claimant and insurance claim.

The physical access path between Claimant and Insurance Claim physical files is shown in Figure 4.20. Each claimant can have many insurance claims, but each insurance claim belongs to only one claimant.

Defining Physical Files

The physical data access chart is developed from the data entity model. A data entity usually becomes a physical file. However, data entities may also be combined to form a single file, or a data entity may be split into several physical files.

This decision is made by reviewing the physical operating environment and the specific characteristics of each data entity, its attributes, and the access paths between entities. It is beyond the scope of this book to discuss all the database management systems and physical operating environments.

When the physical files have been defined, the access paths between those files can be identified. As mentioned earlier, many-to-many relations do not constitute an access path. Therefore, only one-to-many relations can be used for access paths.

Each one-to-many data relation from the logical data relation chart is placed on the physical data access chart. Figure 4.21 shows a logical data relation chart for a relationship between doctor and patient. The many-to-many relation between doctor and patient is resolved by a transaction entity for visit.

The physical data access chart for the relationship between doctor and patient is shown in Figure 4.22. The only access paths are between Doctor and Visit, and between Patient and Visit. There is no access path between Doctor and Patient.

If an entity has been split into two physical files, an access path is shown for both of those files. Figure 4.23 shows a logical data relation chart for attorneys and clients. Each attorney has many clients.

The amount of data stored for an attorney is too large for one record, and the personal data about an attorney is used far less than the professional

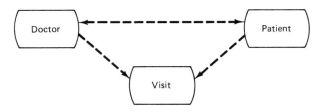

Figure 4.21 Logical data relation chart for a doctor–patient relationship.

Figure 4.22 Physical data access chart for the doctor–patient relationship.

Figure 4.23 Logical data relation chart for attorneys and clients.

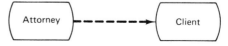

data. Therefore, attorney data is split into an Attorney Personal file and an Attorney Professional file, as shown in Figure 4.24.

An access path is shown between each attorney file and the client file. A one-to-one access path is shown between the two attorney files since both constitute the attorney entity. This access path does not indicate a many-to-many relation. It only indicates an access path which is a one-to-one relation. Each Attorney Personal record has a corresponding Attorney Professional record.

If data entities are combined into a single physical file, the access paths between the combined entities are not shown. The access paths from other entities to the combined entities are shown to the single physical file. Figure 4.25 shows a logical data relation chart for student, address, and class.

Since a student has several addresses, and those addresses are frequently accessed with student data, the addresses are combined as multiple occurrences

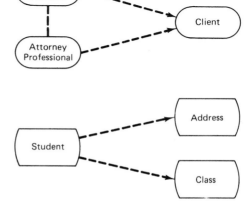

Figure 4.24 Physical data access chart for attorney and client.

Figure 4.25 Logical data relation chart for student and class.

Figure 4.26 Physical data access chart for student and classes.

with the student file. Figure 4.26 shows the physical data access chart for students and classes.

If it is helpful for understanding the physical data access chart, the combined data entity names can be listed in the oval representing the physical file. However, the name of the physical file should be the name of the parent of the combined data entities.

Caution should be used when combining entities into a single physical file. First, the subordinate entity being combined must not have any subordinates of its own. If it does, it should not be combined because access from its subordinates could become difficult.

Second, the subordinate data entity being combined must not be subordinate to another data entity. If it is, it should not be combined because access from its other parent would be difficult. Also, if there is any chance for a subordinate data entity to have another parent in the future, it should not be combined.

The only data entities that should be considered for combination into a single physical file are transaction-level entities that will never have another parent data entity. They must also be frequently accessed with the parent data entity.

Physical Data Structure

The physical data structure is the data structure of the entire physical database. It shows the physical files and the data items in each file. It shows the contents of each file but not the access paths between files.

A brief physical data structure is shown in Figure 4.27. The Employer data entity became the Employer physical file and the Claimant data entity became the Claimant physical file. Only a portion of the total attributes are shown for each file.

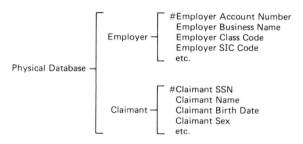

Figure 4.27 Typical physical data structure.

The physical data structure is developed from the logical data structure and the physical data access chart. The physical data access chart identifies the physical files and what data entities were used to compose those files. The logical data structure shows all the attributes that must be defined as data items in these physical files.

The primary and secondary keys from the logical data accesses become keys in the physical files. These are defined by whatever method is available for the particular database management system being used.

A physical data structure showing the placement of two data entities with a one-to-many relation in the same physical file is shown in Figure 4.28. Any wage may have multiple adjustments. The adjustments apply only to the wage, and no other data entity would ever have Wage Adjustment as a subordinate. Also, there is a high frequency of wage adjustment access for each wage access.

For access to this physical file a super-key was created. The super-key is identified by the exclamation mark (!) prefixing the attribute name. The super-key in this case is composed of the three attributes that form the composite key for Wage.

A combination of several data entities, each with a one-to-many relation from a common parent, into one physical file is shown in Figure 4.29. There can be many Disputes, Documents, and Contracts for any one Employer. Collectively, these three data entities represent Compliance activity for an employer. Therefore, they are combined into one physical file termed Compliance.

The composite key is shown for each of the entities in the Compliance file. Since the composite keys do not distinguish between Dispute, Document, and Contract records, a Compliance Record Type is added to each record. A dollar sign ($) is used to identify an attribute added to the physical file that did not exist on the data entity structure.

The database model consists of two submodels: physical data accesses and a physical data structure. This model represents the physical database as

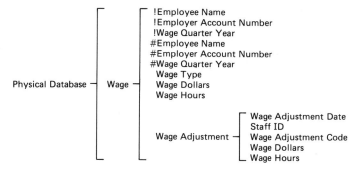

Figure 4.28 Single physical file containing both wage and wage adjustment data entities.

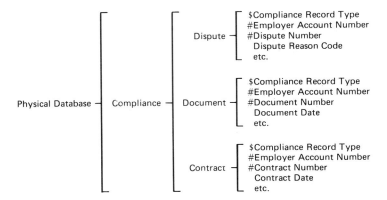

Figure 4.29 Single physical file containing three data entities.

built from the logical database to fit a specific operating environment. It is used both to develop the physical files and as documentation of the physical database.

The physical data accesses show the physical files and the access paths between them. It does not show all data relations between files, nor does it show the contents of any file.

The physical data structure shows the data items that comprise each physical file. Super-keys and any additional data items unique to the physical file are also included.

The database model is developed from the data entity model and specifications about the physical operating environment. Since it is used for documentation as well as design, it must be kept current with the physical database. If it is not current, the chances for a database failure are greatly increased.

SUMMARY

A model is a miniature representation of a system and its elements. In the information-processing field, the systems are information systems and the elements are data and processes. Those elements must be properly managed for the information system to be successful.

The management of information systems is assisted with design models. These models are used to study the business environment, to plan and develop information systems, and to document those systems after development. Without these models, development of information systems would be more costly and would produce poorer systems.

Four different design models are used for developing information systems. Each has its own purpose in the development process. Each is an independent model, yet all four must be used together to assure a successful system.

The business entity model represents the business environment from the company's perspective. It shows the business entities the company deals with and the business transactions between those entities. It identifies the initial data entities and business activities.

The business information model represents the subject matter of the business. It shows the architecture of processes and data. It is used to examine the business and plan its information needs.

The business entity model starts the development process by identifying data entities and business activities. The business information model continues the process by identifying processes, storages, and data flows. It evolves into a group of data flowcharts that define the detailed architecture of information systems.

The data entity model represents the logical database. It shows the structure of the data entities, and the relations and access paths between those entities. It identifies the logical data storages needed to support the information systems.

The data entity model is developed from the data structures identified on the business information model and data flowcharts. Once the inputs and outputs have been identified, the data structures are prepared for each input and output. These data structures are decomposed to provide the data entities, data relations, and access paths.

When the logical database has been defined, the physical database is developed. The physical database depends on the physical operating environment. The logical model is adapted to fit the operating environment in an efficient manner.

The database model represents the physical database. It shows the physical files and the structure of data in those files. It is used to develop and document the physical database.

STUDY QUESTIONS

1. What is a design model?
2. What benefits do design models provide?
3. What is the difference between a business entity and a data entity?
4. What is the purpose of a business entity model?
5. What does a data entity model represent?
6. What is the difference between a data relation and an access path?
7. What does a database model represent?
8. What is the difference between a logical data structure and a physical data structure?
9. How is the system architecture designed?
10. What types of modifications are made during physical database design?

5

DESIGN METHOD

The method of information system design has been evolving for many years. This evolution has included both the details of design and the scope of design. Each plateau in the evolutionary process has been a better method of design than the preceding plateau.

Earlier design methods dealt with design of source code. Projects were smaller in scope and less complex by today's standards. Hardware was smaller and slower and most of the design effort was oriented toward producing efficient source code.

As design methods evolved, the scope of design expanded to an entire information system. Users became more involved and user requirements were defined before design. With larger, faster hardware, the orientation was more toward design of an information system to meet user needs than toward efficient source code.

Recently, design methods are oriented toward information systems architecture. Systems are designed in great detail before they are constructed, much as large buildings are designed before they are constructed. The system architecture will ultimately integrate all information systems in the company.

The current trend is to build information system models that represent a company's business environment and the information it needs to operate in that environment. This trend has led, in part, to independence between business applications and subject data. Both applications and data are needed for successful information systems.

A method is a logical and orderly procedure for performing a series of tasks. It is a sequence of activities utilizing resources and developing products. It is a collection of tools and techniques that can be used consistently on successive projects.

A design method for information systems is a specific method that produces information systems. It must be precise enough to produce a high-quality product, yet flexible enough to be used on a wide range of projects. It must be applicable to both major system development projects and to transient ad hoc requests.

A good design method will not slow down the development process. It will speed up development by providing a precise, consistent, reproducible sequence of activities that maximizes development productivity. It includes all activities that must be performed and only those activities that have to be performed—and it puts them in the right sequence.

Any successful information system development project must be based on a formal design method. However, it is false reasoning to say that any method is better than no method at all. A poor design method can literally cripple any development effort.

A poor design method can also block the development and use of a good design method. Managers must be aware of the success of the design method being used. That method should be revised or replaced as necessary to provide a successful design method.

A successful information system design method must produce a high-quality system that meets user needs and the business goals of the company. It must maximize the productivity of development and produce an efficiently operating system. It must encourage user participation in the design process.

A successful design method must be complete, consistent, an reproducible. It must enhance communication about system design and lead designers toward resolution of basic problems. It must be analytical where necessary and subjective where necessary.

A successful design method must produce simple, understandable models. It must produce a system architecture that represents the real world it serves. Above all, it must produce a workable solution to the initial problems.

The data-structured database design method is a successful design method. It consists of four design models that are based on three mathematical theories. A formal procedure describes the specific steps for developing the models.

The design method described here pertains specifically to database design. However, it is closely linked with data-structured system development methods. Together they form a successful design method that produces successful systems.

DESIGN THEORY

The design of databases is probably the least understood part of system development. There is a preponderance of literature available on database management systems, database hardware, and future trends. However, there is relatively little literature available on the logical design of databases.

This situation is unfortunate because the best database management system and the fastest hardware are relatively useless without a good, logical database design. A good, logical database design, with proper implementation, will provide a stable, useful database. A good, logical design requires a formal design method based on sound principles.

The data-structured database design method is based on the relational model. The relational model is used because it is the best method for use in a dynamic environment. There is very little question that most companies today are operating in a very dynamic business environment.

The relational model facilitates the design, growth, and evolution of a database. It supports the concept of data independence where data is structured independent of the structure of the processing applications. It enhances the sharing of data by many diverse users, yet assures a stable database.

Three-Schema Concept

Traditional database design is based on the two-schema concept. A schema is simply a data structure. The two traditional schemas are an internal and an external data structure.

The internal schema represents the way data are stored in the computer. It is a physical data structure that is relatively fixed and inflexible. In simple terms, the internal schema is the structure of the physical files.

The external schema represents the way data are used outside the computer. It is a logical data structure that must be relatively dynamic to meet changing user needs. In simple terms, the external schema is the structure of the data required by the application program to meet user needs.

The problem arises when the two schemas are actually implemented. A company's data does not fit one hierarchical data structure. Several different hierarchies of the same data are needed at the same time.

This situation creates a conflict between the need for many dynamic structures of the same data to meet user needs, and an inflexible structure of data in physical storage.

There are only two ways to operate in an environment where this conflict occurs. One way is to perform excessive processing to assemble the correct structure of data as it is needed by the application program. However, this approach contradicts the concept of efficient processing on small, expensive hardware.

The second, more common way is to store data in a physical structure that is close to the requirements of the application. This approach results in faster apparent processing but creates redundant data. As more applications are developed with different structures of the same data, more physical files are created.

This trend increases data redundancy, update inconsistencies, and the maintenance load that is so common today. The only way to resolve these problems is to resolve the conflict with the two-schema concept. The problems cannot be resolved by different, or better, methods of operating under the two-schema concept.

The two-schema conflict is resolved by the addition of a third schema: a conceptual schema. This conceptual schema is a collection of data structures representing real-world situations. It is a logical data file that is a common denominator between the requirements of all user applications and the physical storage of data.

The third schema was developed from, and is supported by, relational theory. It provides for independence between use of data and storage of data. It is the foundation for logical database design.

Relational Model

Relational theory treats data as relations and describes how data should be structured and managed. It is based on mathematics and set theory. It is not based on computer hardware or software.

The relational model is a way of looking at data. It is a representation of data and their interrelations that describes the real world. It consists of a set of rules from relational theory for structuring and manipulating data while maintaining its integrity.

The relational model consists of three parts. The structural part defines relations of data and their interrelations. The integrity part assures that each occurrence of a relation is unique. The manipulative part provides operators for processing relations.

The structural and integrity parts of the model are the topics for logical database design. The manipulative part pertains to physical processing, specifically a database management system. The data-structured database design method deals largely with the structural and integrity parts of the the relational model.

Structurally, the relational model is a collection of relations. A *relation* is simply a two-dimensional table consisting of rows and columns of data. A relation, for all practical purposes, is synonymous with table, flat file, subject entity, and data entity.

A *row* is a line of data in a table. Each row is unique among all other rows and represents a real-world occurrence of a relation. It is, for all practical purposes, synonymous with logical record, homogeneous record, tuple, and occurrence.

A *column* is a column of data in a table. Each column represents a specific characteristic of a row. A column, for all practical purposes, is synonymous with element, data item, and attribute.

A *relationship* is an association or interrelation between tables. It is defined in terms of a one-to-one, one-to-many, many-to-one, or many-to-many relationship. It also designates a logical access path between tables.

Since there are many synonymous words pertaining to the relational model, standard words will be used for describing the data-structured database design method. *Entity*, or *data entity*, will be used to represent a table. *Occurrence* will be used to represent a row in a table. *Attribute*, or *data attribute*, will be used to represent a column in a table. *Data relation* will be used to represent a relationship between tables.

Therefore, in logical database design, data are grouped by entities. Each entity contains one or more attributes which describe the entity. Each occurrence represents a unique real-world existence of an entity and its attributes. A data relation is an association between entities.

The format for displaying the relational model is a data structure. Each set in the data structure is an entity. Attributes are the contents of a set. Data relations are identified by the hierarchy of sets and subsets in a data structure. Each occurrence is identified by a primary key.

A primary key is one or more attributes that uniquely identify each occurrence of an entity. A primary key is still an attribute since it does characterize the entity, but it is an attribute with special meaning. A primary key can be composed of a single attribute, multiple attributes from the same entity, or multiple attributes from several entities.

The integrity part of the relational model assures that each occurrence of an entity is unique. Every attribute is stored in only one entity. Every attribute must be a characteristic about the whole primary key and only the primary key.

The manipulative part of the relational model is a set of operators that manipulate physical data. These operators include: select to retrieve rows, project to extract columns, join to combine tables, intersect, union, complement, etc. They are not important to logical database design and will not be discussed further.

Normalization

Normalization theory is associated with relational theory and defines how data entities are formed to capture their inherent nature, structure, and meaning. It provides rules for aggregating attributes by data entity. It defines how data entities are identified to avoid update, insertion, and deletion anomalies.

An update anomaly occurs when an update is made to the database and the database does not agree with itself. It occurs when different access paths lead to different data for the same update. Simply stated, it occurs when there are redundant attributes in the database.

Generally, redundant attributes exist when an attribute describing a parent entity is included in each occurrence of a child entity. When an update to that attribute is needed it must be made to each occurrence of the child entity

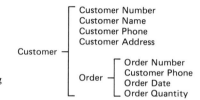

Figure 5.1 Redundant attributes leading
to update anomalies.

rather than just once to the parent entity. This not only causes unnecessary processing, but occurrences of the child entity are frequently missed, resulting in conflicting characteristics about the parent.

For example, a data structure with multiple orders for each customer is shown in Figure 5.1. Customer Phone is stored both in the Customer entity and with each Order for that customer. When the Customer Phone changes, the Customer and all Orders must be changed. If they are not all changed, there are multiple versions of Customer Phone, and an update anomaly has occurred.

An insertion anomaly occurs when an attribute describing a parent entity exists in each occurrence of a child entity but not in the parent entity. A new parent occurrence cannot be completely added when there are no occurrences of the child because there is no place to store the data. That data is lost, which affects the accuracy of the database.

For instance, a data structure with multiple trips for a vehicle is shown in Figure 5.2. Vehicle Year is shown in the Trip entity and not in the Vehicle entity. When a new vehicle is added to the motor pool and has not yet been on a trip, the Vehicle Year cannot be added, resulting in an insertion anomaly.

A deletion anomaly is the reverse of an insertion anomaly. When the last child occurrence for a parent entity is removed, any parent attributes stored with the child are lost. This also affects the accuracy of the database.

Normalization assures that there is no redundancy of attributes and no anomalies. Redundancy is limited to primary keys and their counterpart, the foreign key. Specifically, only foreign keys and composite keys are redundant.

Normalization is accomplished in a series of steps. The initial, or un-normalized form, is the starting point for normalization. The next three forms (first, second, and third normal forms) resolve functional dependencies dealing with single-valued attributes. The last two forms (fourth and fifth normal forms) deal with multivalued attributes.

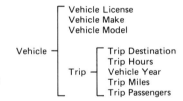

Figure 5.2 Redundant attributes leading
to insertion and deletion anomalies.

Student Number	Student Name	Department Name	Course Name	Course Number
12346	John Smith	Biology	Biology	101
			Zoology	240
			Botany	310
		Chemistry	Chemistry	230
45783	Susan Jones	Biology	Biology	110
		English	Literature	210
			Literature	250
79912	Alice Schwan	Engineering	Mechanics	212

Figure 5.3   Report of classes attended by students.

Data as it is entered, displayed, and reported is considered unnormalized. To be in first normal form all attributes must appear only once in an entity. Or stated another way, all occurrences of an entity must have the same number of attributes.

First normal form is achieved by identifying and isolating repeating groups of attributes. These repeating groups of attributes are identified by the name of the entity they characterize. The data relation between the entities is identified as the groups are isolated.

A partial report of classes attended by each student is shown in Figure 5.3. This report lists student number and name, department name, and course name and number. This report is unnormalized even though it meets a legitimate need of the user.

It should be obvious that there are three repeating groups in this report. The report is for one university and lists many students attending the university. Each student takes classes from many departments. Each department offers many classes.

The data structure for the first normal form is shown in Figure 5.4. Repeating groups of attributes have been identified and placed in their respective entity. The entities have been placed in a hierarchy according to their one-to-many data relations.

Second normal form is achieved by removing partial key dependencies. Each attribute must be functionally dependent on the whole primary key. Each attribute must characterize the whole primary key and only the primary key.

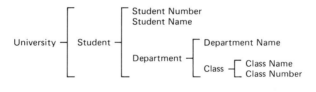

Figure 5.4   First normal form for the report of classes attended by students.

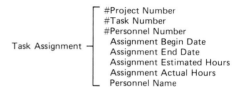

Figure 5.5   Partial key dependency resolved by second normal form.

Task Assignment ┤ #Project Number / #Task Number / #Personnel Number / Assignment Begin Date / Assignment End Date / Assignment Estimated Hours / Assignment Actual Hours / Personnel Name

Partial key dependencies can occur only when there is more than one attribute in the primary key, i.e., compound or composite keys. It cannot occur when there is a single attribute primary key. It usually does not occur if the first normal form is done carefully and primary keys are selected carefully.

The data structure for Task Assignment is shown in Figure 5.5. A project consists of many tasks, and many personnel are assigned to each task. A composite key of Project Number, Task Number, and Personnel Number is needed to make each task assignment unique.

In this example the four Assignment attributes are functionally dependent on the entire composite key. They characterize an assignment as uniquely identified by all three attributes in the composite key. Personnel Name, however, is functionally dependent only on Personnel Number.

To achieve second normal form, Personnel Name must be removed from the Assignment entity and placed in the Personnel entity. When this is done, the Task Assignment entity will be in second normal form.

Third normal form is achieved by removing interattribute dependencies. An attribute cannot be functionally dependent on another attribute in the same entity. If it is, it must be removed and placed in another entity.

The data structure for an employee is shown in Figure 5.6. All four attributes are functionally dependent on the primary key, so the structure is in second normal form. However, Employee Pay Dollars is functionally dependent on Employee Pay Grade; i.e., each pay grade has only one salary.

To achieve third normal form, Employee Pay Dollars must be removed from the Employee entity and placed in an Employee Pay entity as shown in Figure 5.7. When this is done, the Employee entity will be in third normal form.

Figure 5.6   Unresolved interattribute dependency.

Employee ┤ #Employee SSN / Employee Name / Employee Hire Date / Employee Pay Grade / Employee Pay Dollars

Figure 5.7   Interattribute dependency resolved by third normal form.

Employee ┤ #Employee SSN / Employee Name / Employee Hire Date / Employee Pay Grade

Employee Pay ┤ #Employee Pay Grade / Employee Pay Dollars

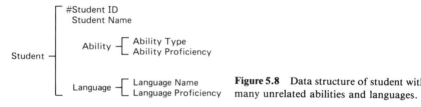

Figure 5.8 Data structure of student with many unrelated abilities and languages.

Fourth normal form is really a specific type of third normal form dealing with how functional dependencies are separated and aggregated. Figure 5.8 shows a data structure for Student showing many abilities, such as reading, writing, and speaking, and many languages, such as French, German, and English. This structure indicates that Ability is related to Student and Language is related to Student, but there is no relation between Ability and Language.

However, if Ability and Language are related, they cannot be separated, as shown in Figure 5.8. They must be combined into the same entity, as shown in Figure 5.9. A Student has many Skills, which consist of related abilities and languages; e.g., a student can speak German fluently.

Fifth normal form deals with reconstruction of dependent attributes from related independent attributes. This reconstruction implies less redundancy of data. However, it could result in additional processing.

Designers should be concerned only about the first, second, and third normal forms. Fourth normal form will occur with a well-thought-out third normal form. Fifth normal form, for all practical purposes, is not currently used in database design.

A good complete third normal form will produce a good logical database and can be achieved if three simple rules are followed. First, attributes must be named carefully and correctly. If attributes are carelessly named, normalization will be very difficult to achieve.

Second, primary keys must be chosen carefully. The primary key must include enough attributes to make each occurrence of an entity unique, but no more attributes than are required for uniqueness. Incomplete, or excessive, attributes will result in less-than-optimal normalization.

Third, the steps for normalization must be executed with precision. Each attribute must be carefully analyzed to determine if it is part of a repeating group, dependent on a partial key, or dependent on another attribute. Assumptions and haste will result in incomplete normalization.

The normalization process is embedded in the development of data struc-

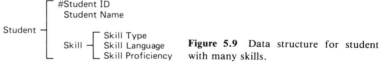

Figure 5.9 Data structure for student with many skills.

tures. The specific techniques for composing data structures are described in Chapter 2. When these techniques are followed, properly normalized data structures will be produced.

Set Theory

Set theory is associated with relational theory and normalization theory. Data-structured database design is supported by set theory in the same way that it is supported by relational and normalization theory. A detailed discussion of set theory is beyond the scope of this book; however, a few basics will help to understand the design process.

When a set F contains elements a, b, c, d, and e, it is shown in set theory notation as

$$F = \left\{ \begin{array}{l} a, b, c, d, e \end{array} \right\}$$

This notation means that set F consists of the five elements shown inside the braces. A set can represent anything and the elements can represent any contents of that set.

In database design the sets are data entities and the elements are attributes. The same notation can be used to represent a set of attributes about the entity Vehicle:

$$Vehicle = \left\{ \begin{array}{l} year, make, model, color, horsepower \end{array} \right\}$$

Year, make, model, color, and horsepower are elements of the set Vehicle, meaning that they are attributes describing the entity Vehicle.

As sets of data get larger, i.e., there are more attributes, this form of notation becomes difficult to handle. A format modification can be made by stacking the elements vertically as shown in Figure 5.10. This notation has exactly the same meaning as that of the horizontal notation above.

A further modification can be made to improve the clarity of the data set. The commas, the right brace, and the equal sign are removed as shown in Figure 5.11. This data structure format convention is used in data-structured database design.

The attribute names are fully qualified by prefixing them with the entity name as shown in Figure 5.12. This naming convention provides a clearly understandable means of identifying the attributes that characterize the Vehicle entity.

$$Vehicle = \left\{ \begin{array}{l} year, \\ make, \\ model, \\ color, \\ horsepower \end{array} \right.$$

Figure 5.10 Vertical set theory notation for data.

Figure 5.11 Modified set theory notation for clarity.

Figure 5.12 Fully qualified attribute names in a data structure.

Nested entities are shown in a similar manner. When a set *H* contains elements *a*, *b*, *c*, *d*1, *d*2, and *d*3, it is shown in set theory notation as:

$$H = \left[\ a, b, c, d1, d2, d3\ \right\}$$

It should be obvious that elements *d*1, *d*2, and *d*3 are a repeating group, i.e., a subset of set *H*.

This hierarchy is shown in vertical notation in Figure 5.13. The equal sign, commas, and right brace have been removed. A subset label *D* has been added for the subset.

This same structure of sets and subsets can be used for data. When a doctor has many patients, patients are a subset of doctor as shown as Figure 5.14. Again, this data structure convention provides an easily understandable format for defining the attributes in the Doctor and Patient entities, and the data relation between doctor and patient.

Since a data structure is in set theory form, although in a modified format, it can be manipulated according to the rules of set theory. Sets can be logically added by a process called *union*, designated by the symbol U. Thus *A* Union *B* provides the logical sum of all the elements in set *A* with all the elements in set *B*.

The common elements in two sets can be determined by a process called

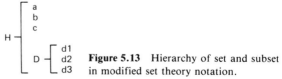

Figure 5.13 Hierarchy of set and subset in modified set theory notation.

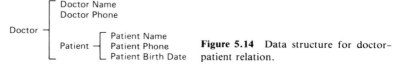

Figure 5.14 Data structure for doctor-patient relation.

intersection, designated by the symbol ∩. Thus $A \cap B$ provides the elements common to both sets A and B.

The difference between two sets can be determined by a process called *difference*, designated by the symbol -. Thus $A - B$ provides the elements in set A that are not in set B, which is also the *complement* of set B that is in set A.

A few other expressions may be useful for understanding the manipulation of data. $A \subseteq B$ means that set A is a *subset* of set B and can have all the elements that set B has. $A \subset B$ means that set A is a *proper subset* of set B and cannot have all the elements of set B. The symbol $\emptyset$ means *null*, which identifies a set with no elements.

These expressions will not be used directly in database design, but they are the rules behind the manipulation of data structures that provide a logical database. They are embedded in the techniques described in Chapter 2. They are presented here so that the reader is aware of what is being done when data structures are manipulated.

Meta-Model

Data-structured database design is based on three associated theories. Relational theory provides a model and a set of rules to define data and their interrelations. Normalization theory provides rules for analyzing data and forming data entities. Set theory provides the rules for manipulating sets of data.

Together these three theories provide the base for a meta-model. A meta-model is the graphic representation, terminology, and rules describing logical database design. Meta-data is the data describing the meta-model.

The meta-model provides a way to design databases that are flexible with respect to the business environment, yet stable with respect to the application programs. These databases are free of storage anomalies, and data redundancy is limited to foreign keys.

The structure of these databases is not predetermined. It is developed from the data required by standard production systems. The structure is then modified to support ad hoc requests.

The databases that are produced have no dependencies between attributes in an entity. All attributes are functionally dependent on the primary key. Navigation between entities is based on these primary keys, and all data can be efficiently updated and retrieved.

This meta-model approach is advantageous because it provides a formal, reproducible method to develop databases. It is simple for analysts, programmers, and end users to understand because it starts with the data they need and ends by providing just that data. The meta-model approach reduces the complexity of the design process and increases the productivity of everyone involved in the design process.

DESIGN PROCEDURE

The data-structured database design procedure is a series of steps that result in a logical relational database which can be implemented into any operating environment. The procedure is based on sound theory, is assisted by design models, and includes a variety of basic techniques. Simply stated, this is where it all comes together.

The design procedure is applicable to major production systems and one-time ad hoc requests. It is applicable to both on-line and batch systems. It is applicable to automated as well as manual systems.

The database design procedure is used in parallel with application design. It is an iterative procedure that produces good business applications and good subject databases. Together, the applications and databases produce successful systems.

The design procedure is output driven with input verification. The outputs are used to determine what subject data storages are needed. The inputs are used to verify that those data storages are properly maintained.

Using only the outputs to determine data storages is not acceptable because there is no assurance that those storages are properly maintained. There is also no assurance that all keys will be identified, since the input access paths are usually different from the output access paths. In addition, the opportunity to identify missing attributes is lost.

Using only the inputs to determine data storages is not acceptable because all the output keys will not be identified. Also, many of the attributes needed for outputs may not be identified. But the worst problem by far is that many unnecessary attributes will be captured and stored.

Using both the inputs and outputs together to determine data storages is not acceptable because it has the disadvantages of both the input-only and output-only approach. Even though all the access paths are identified, it will not determine the data needed for outputs and assure that data is maintained. There could well be data stored that is never used, and data needed that is never stored.

Therefore, the best approach is to determine the data that is needed to support the outputs, then assure that all that data, and only that data, is stored. This is the origin of database design that is output driven with input verification. It has proven best on numerous development projects.

Design Steps

The data-structured database design procedure is, as the name implies, based on the structure of the data. Data structures are prepared for the outputs and are used to define the data storages. Then data structures are prepared for the inputs and are used to assure maintenance of those data storages.

When the inputs maintain all the outputs that are required, the total database is defined. This total database is purely logical, with no constraints from the physical operating environment. When it is completed, the physical database is developed for a specific operating environment.

However, before the data structures can be developed the business environment must be defined and the architecture of the system must be designed. The steps involved in defining the business environment, designing the system architecture, defining the logical data base, and developing the physical database are shown in Figure 5.15. Each of these steps will be explained in detail.

The data-structured database design procedure is based on the design models. The main purpose of these models is to identify and define data entities, data relations between data entities, processes that manipulate the data, and access to the data. Without these design models the design procedure would be very difficult.

Define business environment. Before any business information system can be designed, the business environment where that system operates must be defined. If the business environment is not defined first, the system may not operate effectively. It would be like designing a large building without knowing its location or purpose.

The output of this step is the business entity model. This model identifies the initial data entities, which is the beginning of the data storage definitions. It also identifies the business transactions, which is the beginning of the process definitions. The business entity model is the prelude to designing the system architecture.

The inputs to the business environment definition step are project definition and user knowledge. Project definition sets the scope of the project and the requirements of the system. User knowledge provides the base of knowledge about the business environment.

The business entity model identifies the business entities and the transactions between them. An external model is developed for business transactions between the company and other business entities outside the company. An internal model is developed for business transactions between business entities within the company.

The beginning point for developing the business entity model is to identify business transactions with other business entities outside the company. Project definition sets the scope, and only those transactions within the scope of the project are identified. User knowledge is the base for identifying these business entities and transactions.

If business entity models already exist from a previous project, the new business entities and transactions may be added to these models. If the models do not exist, they can be developed for the current project and enhanced on future projects. The business entity models are constantly enhanced to represent the business environment.

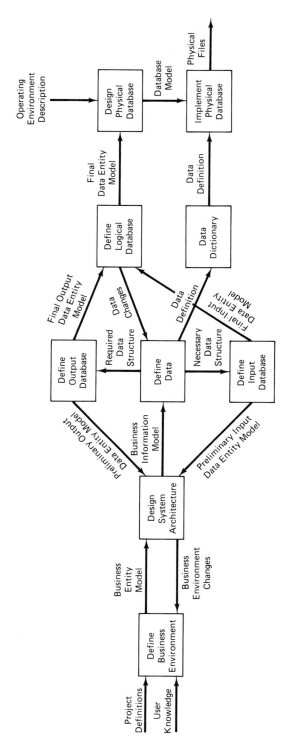

Figure 5.15 Data structured database design procedure.

As business entities and transactions are identified, they are uniquely named and described. This is necessary to prevent redundant or unclear naming and to add meaning to the model. A data dictionary should be used to control the names and describe the entities.

When all business entities and transactions outside the company have been identified and described, the internal entities and transactions can be identified. The external transactions are not shown on the internal model. They have already been described and would only confuse the internal model.

A common approach to identifying business entities and transactions is to start with the most frequent transactions. As these common transactions are identified, the less frequent transactions can be identified. As each transaction is identified, the business entities processing those transactions can be identified.

A common problem in developing business entity models is trying to identify all business processes and all data entities. This is not the purpose of the business entity models. The models are used to identify business transactions that will eventually be used to define all the processes and to identify initial data entities that will eventually be used to define all the data storages.

The best approach is to describe the business environment outside the company first, then the environment within the company. The most frequent business transactions are identified first, followed by those that are less frequent. Direct user involvement is mandatory for development of a complete, accurate business entity model.

Design system architecture. When a good, accurate business entity model has been developed, the architecture of the system can be designed. The architecture shows the structural arrangement of all the elements of a system. The basic elements are processes, data storages, and data flows.

The output of the system architecture design step is the business information model. This model identifies the specific processes, data storages, and data flows necessary for the system to operate. It is the starting point for defining the process logic and the logical database.

The business information model can be defined in greater detail. The levels of detail below the model itself are detailed data flowcharts. The business information model is actually the highest-level data flowchart for the system.

The input to this step is the business entity model. The business transactions are used to develop the business information model. The names of the business entities and transactions are the initial data entity names.

The business environment is event driven. The basic business events are "arrival of an input" or "demand for an output." Each of these events requires an activity to process the event.

The business transactions from the business entity model are the events.

An incoming transaction is the "arrival of an input." An outgoing transaction is the "demand for an output."

The business transactions are taken, one by one, and activities are designated for processing that transaction. The external business transactions are selected first because they show major inputs and outputs for the company as a whole. The internal business transactions are selected last because they correspond to detailed internal transactions.

The sequence for selecting transactions is outgoing transactions first, progressing to incoming transactions. Within this sequence, the most frequent, highest-volume transactions are selected first, progressing to the less frequent, low-volume transactions.

The activities become processes on the business information model and the business transactions become data flows. Data storages are added as necessary to hold data between processes. The processes, data flows, and data storages are arranged according to the rules for developing data flowcharts.

The detailed procedure for building a business information model from transactions is difficult to describe. It requires considerable thought and in many cases considerable trial and error. Many architectural alternatives may be tried before the best architecture is found.

During the development of the business information model there may be changes in the business environment. These changes may result from external sources or from an internal decision to do business a different way. They may even result from a better definition or a clarification of the existing environment.

In any case, these changes must be fed back to the business environment definition step. The business entity model is enhanced and, in turn, provides updated input to the system architecture step. This is an iterative process that leads to complete models for the business environment and the system architecture that are in agreement with each other.

The business information model is the architecture for the total system. It is the point where the development of process logic diverges from the development of subject databases. It is the beginning of data independence.

Define data.   When the business information model is complete, the definition of data can begin. Data definition includes both the description of each attribute and the structure of these attributes. The structure of the data will be used to define both the structure of the process logic and the structure of the database.

The output of this step is a collection of data structures representing all the data flows on the business information model. These data structures will be used to define the input and output databases and the logical database. The logical database will be used to develop the physical database.

The data definition step interacts with the data dictionary. As data entities and attributes are identified, the data dictionary is consulted. If the attribute is already described, its name is used. If it has not been described, the new description is entered according to the rules for naming data attributes.

The input to the data definition step is the business information model. This model identifies all the data flows in the system. It must be complete and accurate if the data structures are to be complete and accurate.

A data structure is created for each data flow on the business information model. Generally, data structures are developed for the outputs first, followed by data structures for the inputs. Although this is not a requirement, it is usually done because the outputs are used to define the data storages and the inputs are used to verify the maintenance of the data storages.

The rules for developing data structures must be followed for each data structure. Paired output and required data structures are developed for each output, and paired input and necessary data structures are prepared for each input. The required and necessary data structures are used for database design, while the output and input data structures are used for developing process logic.

It is extremely important that the data structures be prepared correctly. If their structure is incorrect or the attribute names are incorrect, the database and the process logic could be incorrect. This will cause problems when the source code attempts to access the physical files.

The paired data structures are the precise point of divergence of subject data and application logic. This is the point where the development of process logic goes a separate route from the development of databases. This is the most critical part of the system development process.

The point of convergence of process logic and subject data is during testing. Source code will have been developed from the process logic, and data files will have been developed from data storages. Testing is the first time when the application logic attempts to access the physical files.

If there were errors in the data structures, these errors will be propagated through the development of application process logic and database development. Testing will not be successful and the process of debugging will begin. Since debugging is costly, and largely unnecessary, it is best avoided. The best way to avoid debugging is to develop completely accurate data structures.

The rules for developing data names must be followed. If the rules are not adhered to stringently, synonymous attributes will be defined. These synonymous attributes are a very subtle and devastating form of data redundancy that leads to anomalies.

However, the opportunity never arises to experience update, insertion, or deletion anomalies. What happens is that data is stored by one attribute name and is retrieved by another attribute name. Since separate attributes become separate data items in a record, the data item stored is not the same data item that is retrieved.

In addition to following the rules for naming attributes, the data dictionary must be kept current. If the rules are followed but the dictionary is not updated, synonyms are developed by default. This results in the same problems mentioned above.

The best way to develop complete, accurate data structues is to follow the rules for naming data and for developing data structures, and to keep the data dictionary current. This assures that process logic and data storages will be correctly defined and that testing will be successful. Successful testing means no debugging, which leads to a successful, productive development effort.

Define output database.   When the output and required data structures represent the outputs completely and accurately, the output database can be defined. This step identifies the data entities and the attributes in each entity needed to support the outputs. The data entities, in turn, identify the logical data storages.

The outputs of this step are output data entity models. A preliminary model is developed for verifying or correcting the system architecture. When the verification is complete, the final model is used to develop the logical database.

The inputs to this step are the required data structures from the data definition step. These data structures are decomposed by entity and the attributes are logically aggregated by entity. The result is a collection of entities with their attributes that meet the output requirements of the system.

The process of decomposition is relatively simple. Each required data structure is taken, one at a time, and the entities are decoupled. After each entity is decoupled, its attributes are aggregated into a master data entity for that subject.

As each required data structure is decomposed, the keys required for access to each entity are recorded. A master list is maintained for each unique key group for each entity. This list contains all the access paths required for each entity.

A master list of data relations is also prepared during the decomposition process. This list contains all the one-to-many data relations that occur between entities. It will be used to draw the data relation chart and to identify many-to-many data relations.

The rules for data structure decomposition must be followed. If the decomposition and aggregation process is not done correctly, attributes, key groups, and data relations may be in error. When this occurs, the testing step will fail and debugging will begin.

When all the required data structures have been decomposed, all the logical data storages will have been identified. These data storages are compared to the data storages identified on the business information models. If the model was designed properly, all the data storages identified during decomposition will be shown on the model.

If there is a discrepancy, that discrepancy must be resolved. The resolution could be a change in data structures, a change in the system architecture, or both. Either way, the discrepancy must be resolved.

If the data structures are changed, the decomposition process is performed again. The new logical data storages are compared to the business information model for possible discrepancies. This entire procedure is repeated until all discrepancies are resolved.

One way to assure that this repetitive process is kept to a minimum is to review each required data structure with the business information model as it is finalized. There must be a data flow to or from a data storage for each entity on the required data structure. If not, a change should be made prior to decomposition of the data structures.

Define input database. When the preliminary output data entity model matches the business information model, the inputs can be used to verify that the data storages are properly maintained. This step also assures that each entity on the inputs is represented on the business information model. It is a process very similar to the output database definition step.

The outputs of this step are the input data entity models, which are similar to the output data entity models. A preliminary model is used for comparison with the business information model. A final model is used by the total database definition step.

The decomposition process is the same as described for the output database definition step. Each necessary data structure is taken, one by one, and the entities are decoupled. The attributes are aggregated to a master entity with the same name.

The same rules for data structure decomposition are followed. A list of data relations and key groups is also maintained. The result is an input data entity model that can be compared to the business information model and to the output data entity model.

The preliminary input data entity model is compared to the business information model the same as for the output data entity model. The comparison may result in changes to the inputs, the outputs, or the business entity model. Depending on the type of change, the inputs or outputs may need to be decomposed again.

This iterative process of comparing inputs, outputs, and business information model is repeated until all entities from the inputs are balanced with all entities from the outputs, and these are balanced with all data storages on the business information model. If the data structure charts were prepared correctly and the business information models were designed correctly, the iterations will be few. If they were not done correctly, the iterative process will continue until the data structures and business information model balance.

When the data entities and data storages are balanced, the attributes in each entity are compared. The same attributes must appear in both the input entity and the output entity. If not, there is a discrepancy that must be resolved.

When there is a discrepancy, it indicates that data is stored and not used, or is used but not stored. The discrepancy must be resolved by adjusting the input attributes or the output attributes, or both. If the discrepancy is not resolved, testing will fail and debugging will begin.

Each correction to a data structure requires another decomposition and another comparison. When the comparison shows that the input and output attributes match, the total database can be defined.

Define logical database.   When the output data entity model and the input data entity model match each other and match the business information model, a total data entity model can be defined. This model is developed by adding the two submodels together. The total model represents the total database for the system.

The output of this step is a final data entity model for the system. It identifies all the data entities, and their attributes, data relations, and all the access paths for each entity. This model will be used to design the physical database.

The inputs to this step are the final input data entity model and the final output data entity model. These two models are combined to produce the total data entity model.

The combination process is relatively simple. Since the input entities and attributes match the output entities and attributes, there is no need to combine them. Either one represents the total collection of entities and attributes.

The input data relations need to be combined with the output data relations to produce a list of all data relations for the system. This is done simply by adding the two lists of data relations. All the subordinate entities from the input data relations and all the output data relations are listed for each parent entity.

The input and output data accesses are combined in a similar manner. The unique key groups from the input data entity model and from the output data entity model are listed for each entity. This provides a master list of all access paths for each entity.

The data relations and data accesses are usually different for the inputs than they are for the outputs. This is quite reasonable because the outputs require more mixing and matching of entities to produce the output. Inputs are usually simpler because each input directly updates fewer entities.

Before the physical database is designed, it is preferable to make a final check of the logical database. This final check is made by reviewing the structure of entities and attributes, by reviewing the access paths, and by reviewing the data relations. This is largely a subjective check to determine if the final data entity model is reasonable.

Each one-to-many data relation should be reviewed to determine if it is reasonable. Each child entity is checked to determine if it is a reasonable subordinate to the parent entity. If not, there is a discrepancy to be resolved.

Each many-to-many data relation should be reviewed to assure that it is reasonable. If it is reasonable, a check should be made to determine if there is a common entity that resolves the many-to-many data relation. If not, there is a discrepancy that needs to be resolved.

The attribute names should be reviewed for each entity. If the entity is a basic entity, all attribute names should begin with the entity name, except for foreign keys. If the entity is a transaction entity, the attributes should be reviewed to determine if it is reasonable for those attributes to be in that transaction.

Each data access should be reviewed to determine if it is reasonable. Are all the attributes needed for access and are the attributes in the right sequence? If not, there is a discrepancy to be resolved.

Each of these discrepancies must be resolved before the physical database can be designed. These resolutions may mean changes to the data structures or even to the business information model. When these changes are made, the sequence of decomposition and comparison must again be made to assure that the logical design is correct.

Design physical database.　　When the logical database has been completed, the physical database can be designed. This design adapts the logical database to the physical operating environment. The result is a physical database that can be implemented.

The output of this step is a database model. It shows the structure of the entities and attributes as they will be physically implemented. It also shows the physical keys that need to be defined to allow access to the data.

The inputs to this step are the final data entity model and a description of the operating environment. The final data entity model is the logical database to be adapted to the physical environment. The description of the operating environment provides the specifications about the hardware, software, and database management system where this system will be operating.

It is beyond the scope of this book to describe all of the considerations for designing the physical database. There are too many environments and variations. However, a few general guidelines are available.

Ideally, each subject entity should become a separate physical file. However, this is not always practical or efficient. Multiple data entities could be put into one physical file, or one data entity could be spread across several physical files. Multiple data entities on one physical file can be either parallel or nested.

If several data entities are put into one physical file as parallel entities, there should be a very close tie between those entities. There must be a high frequency of accesses to the multiple entities at the same time. If this situation does not exist, there is no reason to have multiple entities on the same physical file.

If data entities are nested on the same physical file, there must be a close tie between those entities. The subordinate entity must not have any other parents, or even have a likelihood of other parents. There must be a high frequency of access to both parent and child entities at the same time. The child entity should have a relatively small number of attributes.

If these conditions do not exist, the nested data entity should not be on the same physical file. If it is, there could be severe performance problems, depending on the particular operating environment.

Multiple physical files for one entity are used when the number of records exceed the capacity of one physical file. They can also be used when recovery time for a large file becomes unreasonable and smaller files would be more reasonable. A third use occurs when updates are faster with smaller files.

The sequence of data items in a record generally depends on their frequency of use. The most frequently used data items are placed at the beginning of the record and the least frequently used are placed at the end of the record.

Generally, data items that have a low frequency of occurrence are grouped together. These items will probably be suppressed in the record, and grouping will improve the suppression. However, the frequency of use and the frequency of occurrence may have to be evaluated before a final decision is made.

Key groups may be defined as super-keys by whatever mechanism is available. Generally, keys and super-keys are placed at the end of the record because of their low frequency of use. If the key is used to get the record, the key does not have to be retrieved; thus it can be at the end of the record.

The duration of the data item may be considered when placing that data item in the record. Data items with short duration are generally placed at the end of the record. However, the duration of the data item, the frequency of use, and the frequency of occurrence must be evaluated before a final decision is made.

The purpose of the physical database design is to optimize response time, throughput, recovery, performance, and storage space, yet not destroy the relational nature of the data. This often requires a first-cut physical design with optimization based on actual performance statistics. Technical personnel with expertise in this area should be consulted.

Implement physical database.   When the physical database design is complete, it can be implemented. The implementation step uses the physical design and the data definitions to develop the physical files. These files are then available for use by the application programs.

The outputs of this step are the physical files. The inputs are the database model and the data dictionary. They supply the structure of the files and the format of the data items that are used to develop the physical files.

The actual process involved in this step is highly dependent on the specific database management system and the specific data dictionary. It is impossible to cover all the possibilities. Personnel having knowledge and skills with the specific products should be consulted.

Implementation of the physical files is the point of convergence of the application logic and the subject data. The source code will have been developed from the process logic. The process logic was developed from the input and output data structures.

The physical files have been developed from the database model. The database model was developed from the required and necessary data structures. If the paired data structures were developed correctly and the database model was prepared correctly, the physical files should provide the data needed by the process logic. An actual test will determine if the source code can actually access the physical files.

Proof of Correctness

"How is correctness proved?" has been asked more times than any other single question in data processing. It has been answered fewer times than any other question in data processing.

Ideally, any information system going into production should be free of all errors and should be correct in every detail. Traditional testing will show only the presence of errors, not an absence of errors. Lack of errors during testing does not prove correctness.

Correctness is difficult, but not impossible, to prove. Proving correctness follows the premise that prevention is better than cure. If errors can be prevented from entering, they will not have to be removed, and removal is more costly than prevention.

Prevention begins with development of the business entity model. From that step to development of the physical files, errors are prevented from entering. Errors that do enter must not be allowed to remain longer than necessary.

Proof of correctness begins by determining what causes errors. Throughout this book the causes of errors and failures have been explained. Once the causes are known, errors can be prevented from entering, and errors that do enter can be removed quickly.

The proof-of-correctness process identifies errors that enter. One set of proof criteria is provided for each step of database design. When the proof criteria are met, true correctness can be approached.

The database design procedure consists of eight steps, which lead from a description of the business environment to the development of physical files that store data about that environment. Each of these steps requires inputs from a previous step and provides outputs used by a subsequent step. The tasks in each step must be performed correctly, or the physical files will not provide the correct data.

The database design proof of correctness is a series of questions that must be answered. If the answers are affirmative to each question, the database design will be correct and the physical files will provide the data needed by the application program.

The proof-of-correctness questions are listed for each of the eight database design steps. These questions must be answered for each step, not once at the end of design. If the answer to one or more of the questions is negative, a correction must be made before proceeding to the next step.

Define business environment

1. Are the business entities and transactions within the scope of the project?
2. Have all the business entities and transactions pertinent to the project been identified?
3. Have both an external and an internal business entity model been developed?
4. Are all the business entities composed of people?
5. Are all the business transactions flowing between two, and only two, entities?
6. Are the business transactions unique to either the external or the internal business entity model?
7. Have all the feedback changes from the system architecture step been made?

Define system architecture

1. Does the business information model include all business transactions identified on the business entity model?
2. Does the business information model follow all the rules for developing data flowcharts?
3. Have all the changes to the business environment been fed back to the environment definition step?

Define data

1. Are all attributes named according to the naming rules?
2. Are all attributes described in the data dictionary?
3. Have output and required data structures been prepared for each output?
4. Have input and necessary data structures been prepared for each input?

5. Were the rules followed for composing data structures?
6. Have all synonymous attributes been identified and resolved?

Define output database

1. Was each required data structure decomposed correctly?
2. Was each key group properly recorded?
3. Was each data relation properly recorded?
4. Do the entities on the output data entity model match the data storages on the business information model?

Define input database

1. Was each necessary data structure decomposed correctly?
2. Was each key group properly recorded?
3. Was each data relation properly recorded?
4. Do the entities on the input data entity model match the data storages on the business information model?
5. Do the attributes on the input data entity model match the attributes on the output data entity model?

Define logical database

1. Were the data accesses combined correctly?
2. Were the data relations combined correctly?
3. Were the one-to-many data relations reasonable?
4. Were the many-to-many data relations reasonable?
5. Did each many-to-many data relation have a common entity that resolved the many-to-many relation?
6. Were the attributes in each entity reasonable?
7. Were the access paths to each entity reasonable?
8. Are all the access path attributes necessary and in the right sequence?

Design physical database

1. Is each subject entity accounted for on the database model?
2. Is each attribute accounted for on the database model?
3. Is the design optimum for the specific operating environment?
4. Have the data entities or their data relations been altered?
5. Has each access path been defined?

Implement physical database

1. Were the files implemented according to the database model?
2. Were the physical keys defined according to the database model?
3. Were the data items defined according to the data dictionary?
4. Was the testing successful?

The questions appear quite simple and match the tasks in each design step. It is easy to ignore these questions and assume that each step was performed correctly. However, the potential time loss may be more than the time needed to perform the proof of correctness.

The proof-of-correctness criteria will approach verification of true correctness. The final proof of any system is that it meets the user needs. If it does not meet the needs as defined, it is not a successful database design.

Documentation

Documentation traditionally is the last item to be accomplished—if it is accomplished at all. Frequently, it is not done to save time or expense on a project that goes over time and budget. Frequently, it is done quickly and incompletely so that the development effort can be considered complete.

After-the-fact documentation is difficult because it requires remembering what was done. The task is made even more difficult when databases involve considerable detail and frequent changes.

Most people do not have the capacity to remember all the details of a database design. This capacity to remember is hindered by a design that undergoes frequent changes, particularly if the changes are made due to an incomplete design.

A database developed with poor or incomplete documentation will perpetuate itself. Poor or incomplete documentation will not be referenced for maintenance or upgrade. Nor will it be upgraded following an enhancement effort. This leads to a more detailed database that still is not documented.

To avoid this problem, documentation must be completed as each step is completed. If documentation is produced as a natural product of each step, there will be no need for after-the-fact documentation. If documentation is required but is not a natural product, it will be left until the end of the project.

Data-structured database design produces documentation as a natural product of each step. All working documents become documentation, and no documentation is required that is not a working document. As a result, documentation is ongoing with the design process.

In data-structured database design, each enhancement to the database is considered another version of design. Each version follows the entire design sequence and produces upgraded documentation. Emergency maintenance may be performed as required, but that emergency initiates subsequent enhancement that follows the design method and produces upgraded documentation.

The documentation produced in data-structured database design includes the business entity model, the business information model, the data entity model, the database model, data structure charts, and attribute descriptions. These are the pieces of documentation that are maintained. No other documentation is produced by the design method, and no other pieces of documentation need to be maintained.

DESIGN CONCEPTS

The database design procedure provides a series of steps to develop a physical database based on the needs of the business environment. This procedure provides the detailed tasks of each step needed to implement a database. A variety of tools and techniques is available to support each task.

This design procedure can be applied in many different ways in a company. It can be used to promote a variety of business functions. It can be used to support design concepts selected by a company.

These design concepts include data independence, interfacing and retrofitting systems, and prototyping. They include how to develop code and parameter tables and how to evaluate the duration of data retention. They include how to deal with pieces of a large system and how to combine systems into super-systems.

These design concepts do not change the details of the database design procedure. They enhance the procedure by showing how it can be applied to meeting the company's development goals. When these goals are set and the procedure is applied to these goals, the productivity of the company will have been improved.

Data Independence

The data-structured database design method emphasizes data independence. Data independence means that the data is structured independent of the structure of the applications. This independence allows the applications to change without affecting the structure of the data, and it allows the data to change without affecting the application.

This concept is sound and is supported by relational theory and the relational model. It is practiced in most progressive companies. However, there is a wide range in the degree with which it is practiced.

The degree of data independence deals with how the database is accessed by the application. A weaker data independence means that the application program is making the access directly to the database. A stronger data inde-

Figure 5.16 Application program making a direct call to the DBMS.

pendence means that the application program is making a generic access through some type of database access routine.

A weak data independence is shown schematically in Figure 5.16. The application program is making a direct call to the database management system. This is a poor practice for several reasons.

First, the programmer has to make all arrangements to set up the access, make the access, and evaluate the response. This requires more training for programmers to become proficient. It also means more training for all programmers to remain proficient.

Second, it increases the maintenance load. Each individual application contains the code to make the access. Any time the access mechanism changes, such as new releases or a new database management system, all the application programs may need to be changed. The greater the change to the database management system and the more application programs there are, the greater the maintenance impact.

Third, there will be more variations in the way accesses are made. In spite of company standards, each programmer will add his or her own traits to the access. This, in turn, adds to the maintenance load.

A stronger data independence is shown schematically in Figure 5.17. The application program is making a call to an access routine. The access routine calls the database management system and returns to the application program.

This type of database access resolves the problems of a direct call access. However, all the specific accesses must be processed by one access routine. In

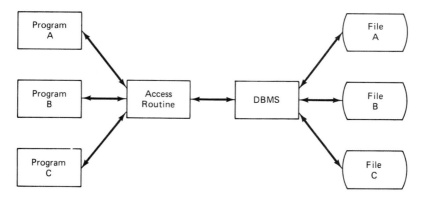

Figure 5.17 Application accessing DBMS through an access routine.

time this routine will become quite large and will itself require considerable maintenance.

A very strong degree of data independence is shown schematically in Figure 5.18. The application program makes a call to an access caller. The access caller, in turn, calls access routines that access the database management system.

This type of database access puts the specific accesses in access modules. The access caller is a communicator between the application program and the access modules. Each access module is unique to only one application program.

This approach reduces maintenance of the access caller by putting the access logic in access modules. The one-to-one relation between application program and access module decreases the maintenance load. When an access is changed, only the application program and its matching access module are changed.

Even when two access modules are initially identical, there is a good chance that they will not be identical in the future. Therefore, the one-to-one relation between application program and access module must be maintained. The only exception is a common access, i.e., to a code table file, where one access could be used for many programs.

The designer has to balance the probability of change against productivity. If there is a high probability of change and a few application programs, the one-to-one relation is maintained. If there is a low probability of change and many applications, a common access module can be used.

The access caller can have varying degrees of smartness. In its simplest form it is essentially a communicator between the application program and the access module. Its purpose is to change a generic access to a database management system specific access.

A smarter access caller will resolve all the changes in the database design

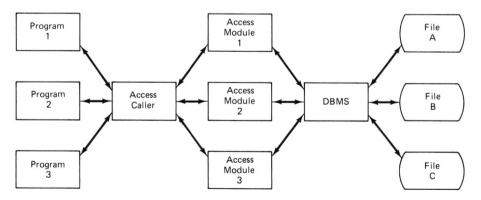

Figure 5.18   Access caller concept for accessing a DBMS.

made between the data entity model and the database model. These changes could be one entity to many files, many entities to one file, or nested entities on one file. Each of these changes added physical parameters to the database model that were not in the logical data entity model.

The application program should request an access via the access caller based on the logical design. The access caller should be smart enough to add the parameters necessary to make the physical access. This leaves the application program completely free of any physical parameters.

The access caller should also be smart enough to access both DBMS files and non-DBMS files. This feature extends data independence beyond the formal DBMS boundaries. It also supports, and helps resolve problems with, interfacing and retrofitting systems.

Data independence is an important design concept in the development of information systems today. It can provide the most benefit when there is a high degree of independence and when the access caller is very smart. The result is reduced maintenance and higher productivity.

System Interface

When a company's managers decide to move into a formal DBMS environment with strong data independence, they are inevitably faced with an interface problem. Any new system developed under new design concepts will not fit nicely with traditionally developed systems. This problem can be severe and cannot be ignored.

A few simple guidelines are available that will help ease the interface problem. There is no way to eliminate the interface problem totally. It must be faced and handled in as productive a manner as possible.

Data flowcharts must be prepared for both the new system and the existing system. Usually, they are prepared for the new system, but frequently they are ignored for the existing system. Even though this appears to save time initially, it sets the stage for severe interface problems.

When the data flowcharts are prepared for both new and existing systems, the interface boundary can be drawn on the charts. This boundary will isolate the specific interface problem areas. Usually, these problem areas are related to data storages rather than processes.

When the data flowcharts are completed, with the interface boundaries, the data structures are developed. These data structures are developed in the same way for both the new system and the interface to the existing system. The only question has to do with what data structures need to be developed.

The data structures that need to be developed are shown in Figure 5.19. A necessary data structure (NDS) is needed for any process, existing or new, that updates a new data storage. A necessary data structure is also needed for a new process updating an existing data storage. A data structure is not needed

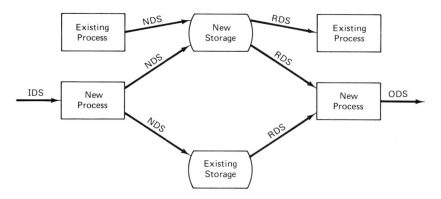

Figure 5.19 Interface data structures to be developed.

for an existing process updating an existing data storage, although it does not hurt to have one.

A required data structure (RDS) is needed for any process accessing a new data storage. A required data structure is also needed for a new process accessing an existing data storage. A data structure is not needed for an existing process accessing an existing data storage, although it does not hurt to have one.

An input data structure (IDS) is needed for any new process updating a data storage. An output data structure (ODS) is also needed for any new process accessing to a data storage. Input and output data structures are not needed for existing applications, although it does not hurt to have them.

When the data structures are completed, a data entity model can be developed. Several iterations may have to be made with possible adjustments to the data flowcharts and the data structures. These iterations will show whether or not there is an interface problem with the data storages.

If there is an interface problem, it can be handled several ways, depending on the type of problem. If a new process needs all or part of the data from an existing non-DBMS file, there is a minimal problem. The access can be made through an access caller for only the logical view desired. It can also be made directly to the existing file for all the data in a record using only the data desired.

If a new process needs more data than is available in an existing non-DBMS file, there is a larger problem. The existing file can be enlarged, or a new file can be created. If the existing file is enlarged to carry the new data, there is a possible impact on existing programs that use and update that file.

If a new file is created, it can be for just the new data not in the existing file, or for the total data. If it is only for the new data, the access caller must be smart enough to combine data to provide a logical view to the application program. If it is for the total data, the access caller must handle both the existing process and the new process. The existing application may need to be changed.

There is no single answer to these alternatives. The impacts need to be analyzed and compared with the long-range plans of the company. The best alternative is then selected.

Generally, it is better to make all accesses through an access caller. The process, existing or new, is then processing only the data it needs. The access caller is deciding where the data is stored and how it is accessed.

This approach allows the physical files to be restructured without affecting the application programs. A file conversion schedule can be established that is less dependent on the application development schedule. The access caller is used to handle the dependencies.

Attribute names can also create a problem when interfacing systems. Usually, existing system attributes are not named by any standard. This creates a problem when interfacing with a new system where attributes are specifically named by rigid standards.

The first step is to identify all attributes from the existing system that are involved in the interface. If there is not a new, well-defined attribute that is the same as the existing attribute, one must be created. The existing attribute is then listed as an alias of the new attribute.

The new, well-defined attributes are used on the data structures. Since the objective is to convert all systems to the well-defined attributes, these attributes should be used as early as possible. The aliases remain as references until existing systems are completely converted and no longer contain old attribute names.

The correction of attribute names should not be ignored. Using poorly defined attributes will only delay the conversion to a solid database environment and create unnecessary problems. If there is any confusion with attribute names, it is best to take the time to define them correctly.

When data flowcharts are developed for both existing and new systems and attributes are correctly defined, the interface problems are reduced. Addition of a smart access caller minimizes the interface problems. This approach allows existing non-DBMS files and new DBMS files to become part of the company's database at the earliest date.

Retrofit Systems

System interface deals with the boundary between new systems and existing systems and the problems associated with that boundary. Many of these problems are resolved, or are at least well defined, by developing data flowcharts and establishing well-defined attribute names. However, this process often uncovers a larger problem.

The larger problem is a high redundancy of data, and sometimes processes, in existing systems. Frequently, this high redundancy was unknown, or only suspected. The use of data flowcharts and well-defined attribute names uncovered this redundancy.

In extreme cases a company may decide to retrofit one or more systems. Retrofitting is the process of applying new technology to existing systems. It is a redesign of existing systems according to current design technology.

Retrofitting can be done in varying degrees. The simplest retrofit is a data flowchart of the existing system with well-defined attribute names. This type of retrofit simply shows how the existing system is operating according to current design technology documentation.

A complete retrofit is a complete redesign of an existing system according to current design technology. It does not include new enhancements to the existing system. It does include making the existing system operate more efficiently.

A complete retrofit is usually not done. When a system is completely redesigned, there are inevitably new features added which were not there before. This exceeds the definition of retrofit and becomes a redesign or a system enhancement.

Occasionally, portions of an existing system that are highly redundant and very inefficient are retrofitted. This is usually done for systems that are not scheduled for major enhancement or redesign in the near future. If a system is scheduled for upgrade and redesign, a retrofit is probably not a good choice.

A complete retrofit means using current technology to redesign an existing system. All the techniques and procedures described previously are used to redesign the existing system. The source of input to the design is the existing system rather than user needs.

The decisions to retrofit must be weighed with other development alternatives and company goals. If a retrofit will meet company goals and fits with the schedule to achieve those goals, the retrofit should be done. If, however, a retrofit is not practical and provides minimum improvements, it should not be done.

Prototyping

A prototype of anything is simply the first of its kind. A prototype system is the first part of an information system. It is the beginning system that is constantly enhanced to meet user needs.

Users generally know their needs and can usually communicate those needs to data processing. However, the user environment is dynamic and user needs are constantly changing to meet that environment. It is a difficult task to keep an information system current to meet the users' changing needs.

In some instances data-processing personnel feel that the user needs are not clear or that the user is uncertain. Data-processing personnel may feel that requirements are not needed, or may even change the requirements. In some cases the users may even be unsure of their needs. These situations lead to system failure.

Two of the problems with system development today are that systems take too long to develop and enhance, and these systems are seldom right the first time. Structured design and direct user involvement have helped to resolve these problems. Prototyping can also be of benefit.

Prototyping is really a feedback loop to the user. It shows them positive results of system development, and it encourages their input into further enhancements of the system. It helps to assure that development is progressing in the right direction.

The prototyping process begins with a simple system. This simple system is refined in successive cycles of improvement based on user feedback. The users have the opportunity to try each cycle and accept or reject it according to their needs.

Generally, the users define their needs for information. A small system is built to perform the most important functions and the user has the opportunity to try those functions. Based on user feedback, refinements are made until the system is completed.

The process is particularly useful when the user needs are truly uncertain. If the users do not know how they want to resolve a problem or how they want to do business, the prototype approach is useful to evaluate alternatives. It will help find the best way to do business.

However, prototyping can be overplayed. It can be used as a means to add new requirements while trying to hold an existing schedule. This approach will cripple the system development effort.

The requirements must be fixed at some point in time. All additional requirements must go to the next version. If the cycles are kept short, priorities are evaluated, and schedules are firm, yet flexible, the prototype approach has value.

Prototyping fits nicely with data-structured development, particularly with database design. Prototype business information models and data entity models can be developed. These models can be evaluated, concurrent with user evaluation of the application, and adjustments or enhancements can be made to the system.

Prototype system design allows an opportunity for corrective action in system development. It allows smaller pieces of the system to be tested and evaluated. When used properly, it will increase the productivity of system development.

Code Tables and Parameter Tables

Codes are used to indicate the status, type, or condition of an occurrence. Many of these codes have an associated verbal description which is considerably longer than the code itself. Actually, codes were originally developed to avoid repeated entry of lengthy verbal descriptions.

In the past, these codes were maintained as independent code tables by the user who owned the data. The users created, maintained, and deleted codes to suit their needs. They did not have to coordinate with, or seek authority from, anyone else.

As applications spread throughout a business and subject databases were created, these independent code tables became a problem. Redundant codes were kept on separate code tables and codes conflicted between code tables. Coordination between users who maintained the code tables was minimal, which made any resolution very difficult.

Also, earlier applications embedded code tables in the program source code. Any change in a code or its description initiated a program change for every program containing that code table. This added to the already mounting maintenance problem, and in many cases programs were not updated.

The combined impact of uncoordinated code tables and high maintenance from embedded code tables was substantially decreased productivity for both users and data-processing personnel. To increase productivity there needed to be a central point of coordination for code table maintenance, and code tables needed to be removed from the source code.

Progressive companies have established a user group, steering committee, or data administration unit to coordinate all code tables. This group reviews and approves all changes to codes from the company perspective and provides a list of current codes to any user. Although this resolves the coordination problem, it does not resolve the source code maintenance problem.

To remove code tables from the source code, a data file is created to contain the current codes and their descriptions. This file is either accessed by the program or loaded into program storage at execution time. Any changes in the codes are automatically available to the program the next time it is executed.

Each code table entity is identified on the required and necessary data structures. These code table entities can be placed on one physical file. That physical file becomes the code table file.

Code tables can be used for encoding or decoding data. Encoding is the process of using the literal description to go to the code table file and retrieve a code. Decoding is the process of using the code to go to the file to obtain the literal description.

Code tables can be used for verification of either a code or a description. To verify a code or a description, the code table file is accessed to determine if the code or description exists. If it does, the code or description is verified. If it does not, it is not verified.

Code tables can be used to determine the next available number in a series, such as next Customer Account Number. The code table file is accessed and the first number is selected for the next customer. That number is then deleted from the file.

In some instances a code can have more than one parameter. These parameters can be stored with the code; however, it could create a slight performance problem. It may be better to establish physical files for two, three, and four attributes for each code.

Another excellent use of the code table concept is the parameter table. In many instances a variety of parameters are fed to a job at execution time. These parameters could be maintained in a parameter file and updated as needed.

Control totals and job statistics can also be maintained in the parameter file or on a separate control file. When a job completes, the control totals and statistics can be entered into the file for future reference. These totals could be the forerunner of a database about the company's business.

Literals, such as report titles and column headings, can be stored in a literal file. Any change in tables or headings could be made to this file rather than to the source code. This would eliminate recompiling programs and it would assure that changes were made to all occurrences of the title or column headings.

The concept of a file for codes, parameters, statistics, or literals will enhance company-wide coordination and reduce program maintenance. Redundancy and conflict will be eliminated. The result is a substantial improvement in productivity.

Duration of Data

The traditional perception of the duration of data is that each data item in a record remains for the life of that record. All data items begin when the record is initiated and cease when the record is deleted. Some data items may be blank initially, but they still exist for the duration of the record.

In the database environment a data item's duration is independent of the record. It may begin at any time, and it may end at any time. Actually, the duration of any record depends on the initiation of the first data item and the termination of the last data item.

During the database design it may be advisable to record the initiation, duration, and termination of each attribute. If there is a wide range of data item durations, this information should be used to design the database model. If the duration of attributes is relatively uniform, there is no affect on the database model.

The same concept can be applied to primary and secondary keys. During database design the initiation, duration, and termination of keys should be recorded. If a key or a super-key has a short duration, it should be generated only when it is needed. When it is no longer needed, it should be destroyed.

These concepts assure that the database contains accurate data and that performance is optimum. Data is entered only when it is needed and is deleted when its usefulness is past. Keys are generated when they are needed and are destroyed when their usefulness is past.

The database is maintaining only data that is needed. Data and keys that are not needed are removed and the space is available for current data. The result is an increase in performance and productivity.

Subsystems and Super-Systems

The database design procedure described earlier pertained to development of a system. However, it is not limited to just a single system. The procedure can be applied to a small portion of a system, or it can be applied to an entire company.

Generally, the design procedure is followed for a development or enhancement project. Projects are usually formed for a system or a part of a system. Projects seldom include several systems.

When parts of a system are combined, it is the data entity models that are combined. The inputs, outputs, and data flow charts have already been compared and balanced in the data entity model. It is a waste of time to combine the necessary data structures and the required data structures and develop a new data entity model.

As systems, or subsystems, are developed using the database design procedure, the data entity models are usually combined. This combined model represents the data entities, data relations, and data accesses for the entire company. The company data entity model is constantly revised as each new system is developed or enhanced.

Occasionally, small projects produce only additional outputs and no new inputs are required. In this situation the output data entity model is compared with the existing data entity model. If all the attributes are available, the input analysis does not have to be performed. If, however, data is required that is not contained on the database, the input analysis must be performed.

The database models are also combined to represent the company database model. However, some caution should be used when combining database models. A routine combination could lead to poor performance.

It is better to use the company data entity model and determine what the database model would be like if it were developed. This database model can be compared to the combined database model for discrepancies. Any discrepancy should be evaluated and resolved.

Usually, the discrepancies that occur are nested entities that acquire another parent. If multiple parents are valid, the nested entity must be removed from its existing parent and placed in a file of its own.

Another discrepancy can be the negation of a close relationship between multiple entities on one file. When this occurs, the entities should be moved to their own files. However, the performance should be evaluated before the change is made.

The important point to remember is that the data entity model is used when working between subsystems and the company at large. The data entity model can be merged and separated as necessary to evaluate the company's database. It is a poor practice to perform the merging and separating based on the required and necessary data structures.

SUMMARY

The data-structured database design method is a formal method for designing and developing databases. The method is flexible and adaptable to a wide variety of design situations, yet is consistent and reproducible. It emphasizes user involvement in the design process.

The design method is supported by three theories. Relational theory, and the relational model, define how data is structured and managed. Normalization theory defines how data entities are formed and described. Set theory defines how data is manipulated.

The design method utilizes four design models for the design and development of databases. The business entity model defines the business environment inside and outside the company. The business information model defines the architecture of the information system that supports the company in that business environment.

The data entity model defines the data structures, data relations, and data accesses for the data storages. The database model defines the physical files that are used to store the data. These are the files that the process logic will access for data storage and retrieval.

The database design procedure consists of eight steps that lead from project definition to implementation of physical files. These eight steps produce the four design models which are part of the permanent database documentation. The design is assured of being successful by precise proof-of-correctness criteria.

The database design method emphasizes strong data independence, minimum data redundancy, and strong data sharing. It can be used for designing new systems, interfacing new systems to existing systems, or retrofitting existing systems. It can be used in a prototype mode where the complete details of a system are not known.

Data-structured database design is used concurrently with application design where a complete logical design precedes physical implementation. It is useful in a dynamic business environment where changes are constantly occurring. When used properly it provides a successful database and optimizes productivity.

STUDY QUESTIONS

1. What is a successful design method?
2. What is the difference between the two-schema and the three-schema approach?
3. How does the relational model view data?
4. What are the three parts of the relational model?
5. What is the normalization process?
6. How do the three storage anomalies differ?
7. How is set theory used in database design?
8. Why is data-structured database design output driven with input verification?
9. What are the steps of the database design procedure?
10. How is correctness proven?
11. What documentation is maintained for data-structured system development?
12. What is involved in strong data independence?
13. What constitutes a smart access caller?
14. How are new and existing systems interfaced?
15. When should a system retrofit occur?
16. What are the advantages and disadvantages of prototyping?
17. What is the benefit of the code table concept?
18. Why is the duration of data important to database design?
19. How are the database designs from several systems combined?
20. Why is logical database design separated from physical database design?

6

CASE STUDY

Any method, whether in information science or in another discipline, is worthless unless it works in the real world. The best method, based on the best theory, is useless if it does not solve the everyday problems. A successful method is one that solves everyday problems effectively and efficiently.

The data-structured database design method described in Chapter 5 was developed to solve the everyday problems of real-world database design. It is based on sound theory and has been repeatedly refined by actual use on development projects. The result is a very successful database design method.

An actual case study is presented to show how the data-structured database design method is used. This case study pertains specifically to information-processing task management. Although it is limited in scope, it does show how the design method is applied.

The case study begins with a description of the business environment and the problems that are encountered with task management in that environment. It progresses through the development of design models, design of the application system, and development of the database. It also shows how process logic accesses the database.

No input or output formats are shown since they have no direct bearing on the database design. Only the data structures are shown, since it is the data structures that are input to the design process, not the actual formats.

Most of the situations encountered in database design are used in the case study. Where possible, variations and options are shown to illustrate how various design alternatives are evaluated. The result is a complete example that shows most of the features of the design method.

When reviewing this case study, the reader should not be overly concerned about the specifics of this particular task management system. The
specifics will vary based on actual needs and are not important. It is the use
of the design method to develop a database that is important.

ENVIRONMENT DESCRIPTION

In the information-processing environment, many requests are received by
information-processing section managers from a variety of requesters. The
requests may be from fiscal, personnel, manufacturing, sales, public relations,
etc., and may range from a request for an additional terminal to one for a
major information system.

When a request is received by the section manager, it is broken into one
or more tasks. These tasks are assigned to various staff people in the section
for completion. The assignment of tasks is based on priority, work load, skill,
knowledge, etc.

Once a task is assigned to a staff person, a task status is required so that
the section manager can track the progress of all tasks. This allows the section
manager to be more knowledgeable about each task and to respond to other
requests, delays, and priority changes. Ideally, it allows the section manager
to be proactive in task management.

In this particular environment the requester is not charged for the service. However, each staff person must turn in time sheets to the section manager. This allows the manager to track time spent on projects so that better
estimates can be provided for future requests.

The problem with the current task management process is that it is paper
bound. Task assignments, task statuses, and staff times are handwritten and
hand delivered. All calculations are performed by hand, if they are performed
at all.

The section managers have a paper nightmare to wade through to find
original task descriptions, current task status, and time expenditures. Response to additional requests and priority changes is slow, and it is difficult
to provide a current status to requesters. In short, task management is reac-
tive, not proactive.

The section managers need an automated system that can be used to
enter each task, track it to completion, and determine the time spent on the
task. The system must provide current, accurate information about each task.
It must also provide current, accurate information about the staff people who
are performing those tasks.

Based on the description of the environment, the business entity model
shown in Figure 6.1 was developed. It shows three business entities involved
in task management: Requester, Section, and Staff. It also shows four business

Figure 6.1 Business entity model for task management.

transactions between those entities: Request, Task Assignment, Task Status, and Staff Time.

Too often the business entity model is made more complicated than it needs to be. For instance, the request may go from the initial requester to the requester's manager, for approval, and then to information systems. The initial requester and his or her manager may even discuss and alter the request before it is sent.

These actions are not shown on the business entity model. They only confuse the issue of task management. The basic business environment is a request for service from the requester to an information system section manager.

Within information systems, various section managers may discuss the request to decide who will be responsible for completion. The information system director may set or change priorities. Various staff people may be consulted before the task is assigned.

Again, these actions would unreasonably complicate the business entity model. The basic business environment is the assignment of a task to a staff person by the section manager. How that task is assigned is not an issue for the business entity model.

If development of the business entity model is faltering, its development should be reviewed. The business entity model shows "what" is happening in the business environment, not "how" it happens. If the "how" is being put on the business entity model, it should be removed.

In the task management system the "whats" are a request from requester to section manager, task assignment from section manager to staff person, and task status and staff time from staff person to section manager. The "hows" of request preparation, task assignment, task status reporting, and staff time reporting are not shown.

The environment description and the business entity model start the design process. The business entities involved in task management and the basic transactions of task management have been identified. These are used to identify the business activities that continue the design process.

OUTPUT DEFINITION

When the business entity model has been completed to the best of the knowledge available, the system design process can continue. The business entity model, however, may not be final. It can be revised through the entire design process to reflect change in knowledge about the environment.

System design continues with a definition of the outputs. These outputs are based on the business activities that are performed. As the business activities are identified and defined, the outputs needed to support those activities are defined.

In the task management system, nine different outputs have been identified to support business activities. Each of these outputs will be defined, including the output and required data structures.

Task Assignment Report

The Task Assignment Report is a weekly listing of all tasks open as of the preceding weekly report or new during the week. One report is produced for the company and tasks are listed by task number. The report is used as an index of all open and new tasks.

The output data structure for the Task Assignment Report is shown in Figure 6.2. Company is the highest-level single-occurrence entity. Run Date is a parameter and the company totals are calculated attributes. The data set for Open or New Task indicates that only open or new tasks are listed.

The required data structure for the task assignment report is shown in Figure 6.3. Since there are many tasks for a requester, and only one requester per task, task is subordinate to requester. The same situation applies to section and staff.

Requester Name is identified as the primary key for accessing Requester. Requester Name is added as a foreign key to Task for access to Requester.

Section and Staff are accessed by Task to obtain Section Name and Staff Name, respectively. Since these names may not be unique, and may change,

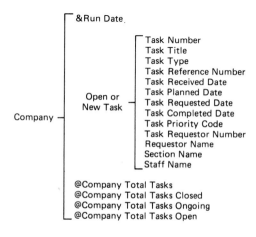

Figure 6.2 Task assignment report output data structure.

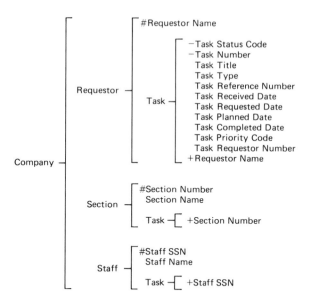

Figure 6.3 Task assignment report required data structure.

Section Number and Staff SSN are identified as the primary keys for access. They are also added as foreign keys to Task.

The task attributes are listed only once. Task Number is identified as a secondary key because it is used to select tasks in task number order. The Task entity within Section and Staff is used to show the subordinate relation and the access.

Task Status Code is added to Task for selecting tasks and calculating company totals. If it were only used for accumulating company totals, it would be identified as a supportive attribute. However, since it is also used for selecting open and new tasks, it is identified as a secondary key.

The data set for Open or New Task has been dropped. It shows only that a subset of all tasks is selected for listing. It has been replaced by the Task set with a secondary key for Task Status Code and Task Number.

The process logic for this report will be Task driven. Open and new tasks will be selected and listed in task number order. The Requester, Section, and Staff entities will be accessed for their attributes needed on the output. Company totals will be accumulated for all tasks.

Task Status Report

The Task Status Report is a weekly listing of all tasks open as of the preceding weekly report or new during the week. One report is produced for the company and tasks are listed by task number. All status descriptions are

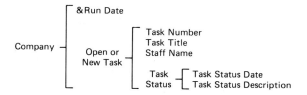

Figure 6.4   Task status report output data structure.

listed in chronological order for each task. The report is used to show the status description and history for open and new tasks.

The output data structure for the Task Status Report is shown in Figure 6.4. Task attributes are listed for each open or new task. Status attributes are listed for all status descriptions for each task.

The required data structure for the Task Status Report is shown in Figure 6.5. Task Number is identified as a primary key for uniqueness and access because Task has a subordinate entity, and it is used to list tasks in task number order. Task Status Code is added to Task as a secondary key for selecting open and new tasks.

Task Number is added as a secondary key to Task Status to select all status descriptions for a task. Task Status Date is identified as a secondary key because it is used to list status descriptions in chronological order.

The process logic for this report will also be task driven. Open and new tasks will be selected and listed in task number order. Staff will be accessed for Staff Name. All status descriptions will be obtained in chronological order for each task.

Staff Time Report

The Staff Time Report is a list of all tasks for each staff person for any desired week, not just for the current week. Tasks having time accrued during that week are listed by task number, for each staff person. This report is used to evaluate a staff person's time.

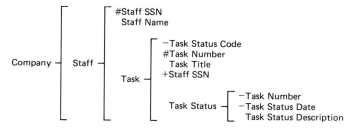

Figure 6.5   Task status report required data structure.

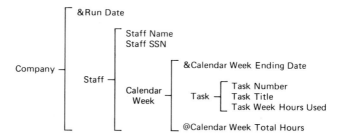

Figure 6.6   Staff time report output data structure.

     The output data structure for the Staff Time Report is shown in Figure 6.6. Calendar Week is shown as a data set within Staff for listing selected tasks. Tasks are selected by the Calendar Week Ending Date parameter. All tasks showing accrued hours for that week are listed.

     The required data structure for the Staff Time Report is shown in Figure 6.7. The data set for Calendar Week has been removed since its attributes are either parameters or calculated. A Task Week set has been added subordinate to Task.

     Staff SSN is used to list each staff person on the report. Staff SSN is added as a secondary key to Task to select all tasks for a staff person. Task Number is shown as a primary key for uniqueness only.

     Task Number has been added to Task Week as a secondary key for selecting all task weeks for a task. Task Week Ending Date has been added as a secondary key for selecting a specific week.

     The Task Week entity is not the same as the Task Status entity in Figures 6.4 and 6.5. A task status can be entered at any time during the week, and there could be no entries or multiple entries during a week. The Task Week entity represents a fixed calendar week with one entry per week if time has been accrued.

     The process logic for this report will be staff driven. The tasks for each staff person will be scanned. If that task has a task week occurrence for the desired week, it will be selected and listed.

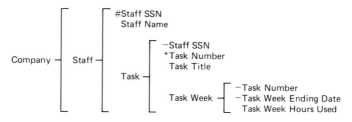

Figure 6.7   Staff time report required data structure.

Section Manager Report

The Section Manager Report is a weekly listing of all tasks open, new, or completed any time during the current calendar year. Tasks are listed by task number for each section. This report is used by the section managers for staff planning.

The output data structure for the Section Manager Report is shown in Figure 6.8. Current Date is a parameter for selecting tasks for the calendar year and accumulating totals. Week, month, and year totals are calculated for each task and for the section.

The required data structure for the Section Manager Report is shown in Figure 6.9. The Calendar Year set is dropped and the Task Week set is added to provide the weekly data for calculating totals. All totals are calculated from Task Week Hours Used.

Section Number is used to list each section on the report. Section Number is added to Task as a secondary key to select all tasks for a section.

Task Status Code is added to Task as a secondary key for selecting open

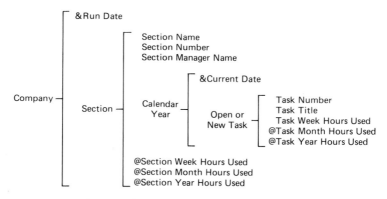

Figure 6.8   Section manager report output data structure.

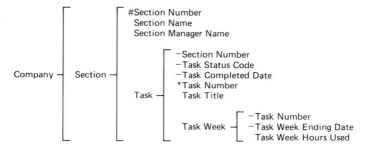

Figure 6.9   Section manager report required data structure.

and new tasks. Task Completed Date is added as a secondary key for selecting tasks completed during the year. Task Number is shown as a primary key for uniqueness only.

Task Number is added as a secondary key in Task Week to select all task week occurrences for a task. Task Week Ending Date is added as a secondary key for obtaining task weeks in chronological order.

The process logic for this report is section driven. The tasks for each section will be scanned. Any task open, new, or completed during the current calendar year will be listed. The week, month, and year totals will be accumulated for the task and for the section.

Monthly Task Report

The Monthly Task Report is a weekly listing of all tasks planned to be completed during the month. One report is produced for the company with tasks listed in chronological order by planned completion date. The report is used to identify all tasks, regardless of section or staff assignment, that need to be completed during the month.

The output data structure for the Monthly Task Report is shown in Figure 6.10. The Month Due set is a data group for all tasks due to be completed during the month. The Month attribute is a parameter for selecting those tasks.

The required data structure for the Monthly Task Report is shown in Figure 6.11. Task is shown subordinate to Requester, Section, and Staff. Requester Name, Section Number, and Staff SSN are shown as the primary keys for accessing their respective entities.

Task Planned Date is identified as a secondary key to select all tasks due during the month. Task Number is not needed as a key for this report. Requester Name, Section Number, and Staff SSN are added as foreign keys to Task.

The process logic for this report will be task driven. Tasks with a Task Planned Date during the current month will be selected and listed in chron-

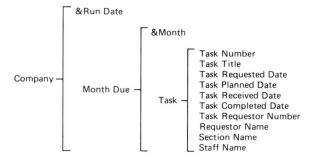

Figure 6.10 Monthly task report output data structure.

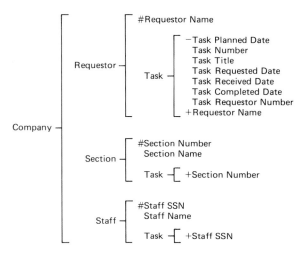

Figure 6.11   Monthly task report required data structure.

ological order by that planned completion date. The Requester, Section, and Staff entities will be accessed for their attributes.

Section Task Report

The Section Task Report is a weekly listing of all tasks for each section regardless of their status. All tasks are listed by task number for each section. This report is used by the section manager to review all tasks for planning purposes.

The output data structure for the Section Task Report is shown in Figure 6.12. Task Hours Used is calculated from Task Week Hours Used for that task. Section Hours Estimated and Section Hours Used are calculated from Task Hours Estimated and Task Hours Used, respectively. Section totals are accumulated by task status.

The required data structure for the Section Task Report is shown in Figure 6.13. Section Number is added as a secondary key to Task to select all tasks for a section. Task Number is a primary key for uniqueness and for listing tasks by task number. Task Status Code is identified as a supportive attribute since it is needed for the section totals by status.

Task Week Hours Used is shown as a supportive attribute in Task Week. It is used to calculate Task Hours Used. Task Number is added as a secondary key to obtain all task week occurrences for a task.

The process logic for this report will be section driven. All tasks for each section will be obtained and listed. All task week occurrences will be obtained for each task to accumulate total hours.

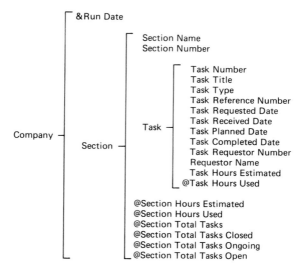

Figure 6.12   Section task report output data structure.

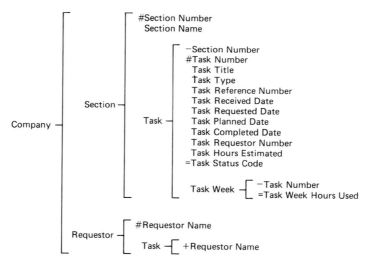

Figure 6.13   Section task report required data structure.

Requester Task Report

The Requester Task Report is a weekly listing of all tasks for each requester regardless of status. All tasks are listed by task number for each requester. This report is used by the requester to review his or her particular requests.

The output data structure for the Requester Task Report is shown in Figure 6.14. Task Hours Used is calculated from Task Week Hours Used. Requester Total Hours is calculated from Task Hours Used. The requester task totals are accumulated by Task Status Code.

The required data structure for the Requester Task Report is shown in Figure 6.15. Requester Name is added as a secondary key to obtain all tasks for each requester. Task Status Code is added to Task as a supportive attribute.

Task Number is added to Task Week as a secondary key to obtain all task week occurrences for a task. Task Week Hours Used is added as a supportive attribute.

The process logic for this report will be requester driven. All tasks for each requester will be obtained and listed. All task week occurrences will be obtained for each task to accumulate total hours. The Section and Staff entities will be accessed for their respective attributes.

Staff Task Report

The Staff Task Report is a weekly listing of all tasks assigned to each staff person regardless of status. Tasks are listed by task number for each staff person. This report is used by each staff person to review tasks assigned to him or her.

The output data structure for the Staff Task Report is shown in Figure 6.16. All tasks are listed for each staff person. Task Hours Used is calculated from Task Week Hours Used. The staff totals are accumulated by Task Status Code.

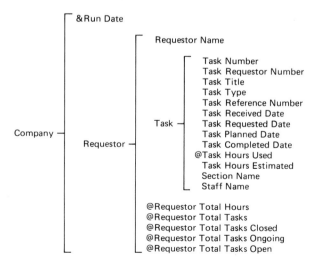

Figure 6.14   Requester task report output data structure.

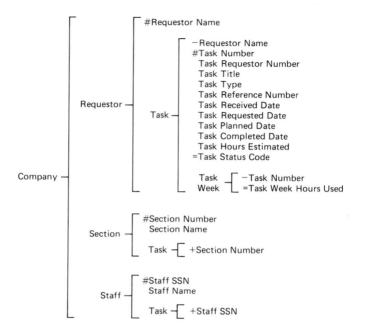

Figure 6.15 Requester task report required data structure.

The required data structure for the Staff Task Report is shown in Figure 6.17. Task Status Code is added to Task as a supportive attribute. Staff SSN is added as a secondary key to obtain all tasks for a staff person.

Task Number is added to Task Week as a secondary key to select all task week occurrences for a task. Task Week Hours Used is added as a supportive attribute to accumulate total hours.

The process logic for this report will be staff driven. All tasks for each staff person will be obtained and listed. All task week occurrences will be obtained for each task to accumulate total hours.

Task Priority Report

The Task Priority Report is a weekly listing of all tasks open as of the preceding week's report or new during the week. One report is produced for the company and all tasks are listed by planned completion date within priority. The report is used by section managers for planning purposes.

The output data structure for the Task Priority Report is shown in Figure 6.18. The Open or New Task data set indicates that only open or new tasks are listed. The Task Priority data set indicates that tasks are grouped by priority. Both Task Priority Code and Task Priority Description are listed.

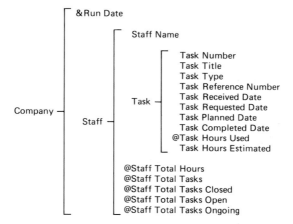

Figure 6.16 Staff task report output data structure.

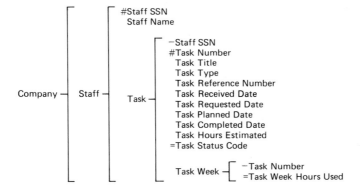

Figure 6.17 Staff task report required data structure.

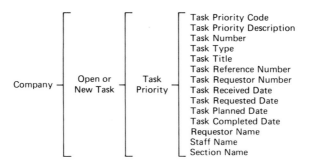

Figure 6.18 Task priority report output data structure.

The required data structure for the Task Priority Report is shown in Figure 6.19. Task is subordinate to the Requester, Staff, and Section entities. Code Table A has been added for obtaining the Task Priority Description.

Task Status Code is added to Task as a secondary key to select new or open tasks. Task Priority Code is identified as a secondary key to obtain tasks by priority. Task Planned Date is identified as a secondary key to list tasks by planned completion date. Task Number is not needed as a key.

Task Priority Code is identified as the primary key for uniqueness and access to Code Table A. The Task set within Code Table A shows that Task Priority Code is used to obtain the Task Priority Description from Code Table A.

The process logic for this report will be task driven. All new or open tasks will be obtained in planned completion date order within priority. The parent entities will be accessed for their attributes.

These outputs were defined by the users of the task management system to support their business activities. They will be used to define the output data entity model. That model will contain all attributes and accesses necessary to meet the output requirements.

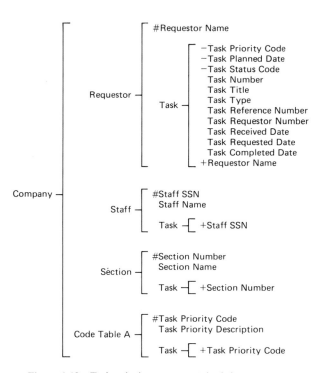

Figure 6.19 Task priority report required data structure.

OUTPUT DATA ENTITY MODEL

The output data entity model is developed from the required data structures. Each required data structure is decomposed and the attributes are logically aggregated by entity. During decomposition the data relations and access paths are recorded.

After Task Assignment Report

The Task Assignment Report required data structure (Figure 6.3) contains four entities: Requester, Section, Staff, and Task. The output logical data structures from this decomposition are shown in Figure 6.20. The aggregated attributes are shown in their respective entities.

The output logical data relations in Figure 6.21 show Task subordinate to Requester, Section, and Staff. Requester, Section, and Staff are all subordinate to Company.

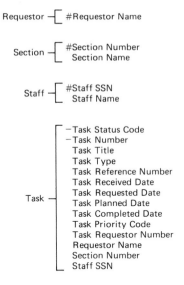

Figure 6.20 Output logical data structures from the first decomposition.

Figure 6.21 Output logical data relations from the first decomposition.

Requestor
    #Requestor Number
Section
    #Section Number
Staff
    #Staff SSN
Task
    —Task Status Code   **Figure 6.22** Output logical data accesses
    —Task Number   from the first decomposition.

The output logical data accesses are shown in Figure 6.22. Requester, Section, and Staff each have a primary key for uniqueness and access. Task has two secondary keys for selecting and sequencing tasks.

After Adding Task Status Report

The required data structure for the Task Status Report (Figure 6.5) has three entities: Staff, Task, and Task Status. Task and Staff have already been identified in the output logical data structures. Task Status is a new entity.

The results of decomposition and aggregation of the Task Status Report required data structure are shown in Figure 6.23. There are no additions to the Requester, Section, Staff, or Task entities. The Task Status entity has been added with its attributes. Task Number within Task has been changed from a secondary key to a primary key for uniqueness and access.

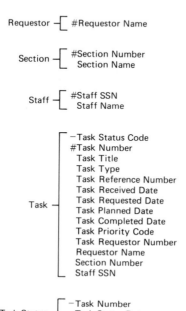

Requestor —[#Requestor Name

Section —[#Section Number
            Section Name

Staff —[#Staff SSN
          Staff Name

Task —
    —Task Status Code
    #Task Number
    Task Title
    Task Type
    Task Reference Number
    Task Received Date
    Task Requested Date
    Task Planned Date
    Task Completed Date
    Task Priority Code
    Task Requestor Number
    Requestor Name
    Section Number
    Staff SSN

Task Status —
    —Task Number   **Figure 6.23** Output logical data struc-
    —Task Status Date   tures from the second decomposition.
    Task Status Description

Company
    Requestor
    Section
    Staff

Requestor
    Task

Section
    Task

Staff
    Task

Figure 6.24 Output logical data relations from the second decomposition.

Task
    Task Status

Requestor
    #Requestor Number

Section
    #Section Number

Staff
    #Staff SSN

Task
    −Task Status Code
    #Task Number

Figure 6.25 Output logical data accesses from the second decomposition.

Task Status
    −Task Number
    −Task Status Date

The output logical data relations are shown in Figure 6.24. Task Status has been added subordinate to Task. No other changes were made to the data relations.

The output logical data accesses are shown in Figure 6.25. Task Number has been changed to a primary key. Task Status has been added with two secondary keys for selecting and sequencing status descriptions.

After Adding Staff Time Report

The results of decomposition and aggregation of the Staff Time Report required data structure (Figure 6.7) are shown in Figure 6.26. Task Week is added as a new entity with its attributes. Staff SSN has been identified as a secondary key within Task.

Task Number is identified as a primary key for uniqueness only in Figure 6.7. However, it already exists as a primary key for uniqueness and access. Therefore, it is not changed.

The output logical data relations are shown in Figure 6.27. Task Week has been added subordinate to Task. All other data relations remain the same.

The output logical data accesses are shown in Figure 6.28. A new access is shown for Task to access all tasks for a staff person. Task Week has been added with its two secondary keys.

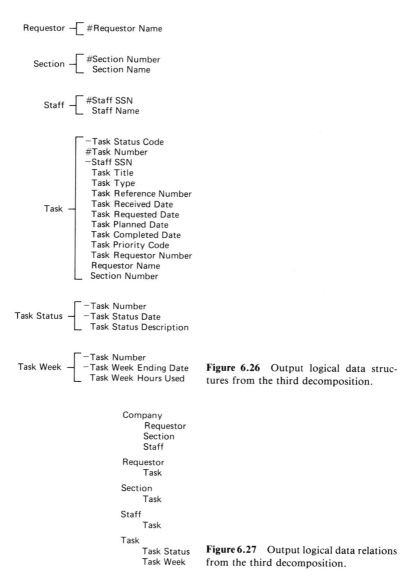

Requestor ⊢ #Requestor Name

Section ⊢ #Section Number
           Section Name

Staff ⊢ #Staff SSN
         Staff Name

Task ⊢
  −Task Status Code
  #Task Number
  −Staff SSN
  Task Title
  Task Type
  Task Reference Number
  Task Received Date
  Task Requested Date
  Task Planned Date
  Task Completed Date
  Task Priority Code
  Task Requestor Number
  Requestor Name
  Section Number

Task Status ⊢
  −Task Number
  −Task Status Date
  Task Status Description

Task Week ⊢
  −Task Number
  −Task Week Ending Date
  Task Week Hours Used

Figure 6.26   Output logical data structures from the third decomposition.

Company
    Requestor
    Section
    Staff
Requestor
    Task
Section
    Task
Staff
    Task
Task
    Task Status
    Task Week

Figure 6.27   Output logical data relations from the third decomposition.

After Adding Section Manager Report

The results of decomposition and aggregation of the Section Manager Report required data structure (Figure 6.9) are shown in Figure 6.29. Section Manager Name has been added to the Section entity. Task Completed Date and Section Number have been identified as secondary keys within Task.

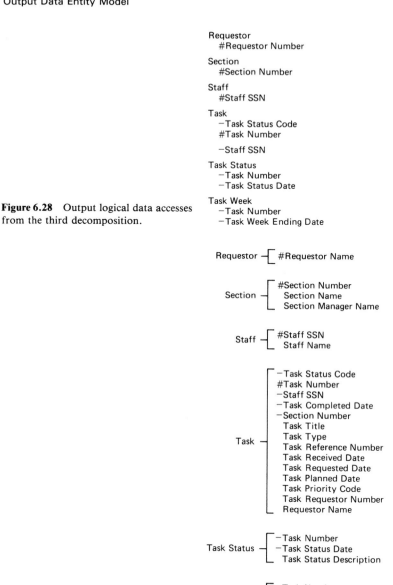

Requestor
    #Requestor Number

Section
    #Section Number

Staff
    #Staff SSN

Task
    −Task Status Code
    #Task Number

    −Staff SSN

Task Status
    −Task Number
    −Task Status Date

Task Week
    −Task Number
    −Task Week Ending Date

Figure 6.28 Output logical data accesses from the third decomposition.

Requestor ─┤ #Requestor Name

Section ─┤ #Section Number
          Section Name
          Section Manager Name

Staff ─┤ #Staff SSN
        Staff Name

Task ─┤ −Task Status Code
        #Task Number
        −Staff SSN
        −Task Completed Date
        −Section Number
        Task Title
        Task Type
        Task Reference Number
        Task Received Date
        Task Requested Date
        Task Planned Date
        Task Priority Code
        Task Requestor Number
        Requestor Name

Task Status ─┤ −Task Number
              −Task Status Date
              Task Status Description

Figure 6.29 Output logical data structures from the fourth decomposition.

Task Week ─┤ −Task Number
            −Task Week Ending Date
            Task Week Hours Used

The output logical data relations shown in Figure 6.27 are not changed. The output logical data accesses are shown in Figure 6.30. A new access is added to Task for selecting and sequencing reports by section for the calendar year.

Requestor
  #Requestor Number

Section
  #Section Number

Staff
  #Staff SSN

Task
  −Task Status Code
  #Task Number

  −Staff SSN

  −Section Number
  −Task Status Code
  −Task Completed Date

Task Status
  −Task Number
  −Task Status Date

Task Week
  −Task Number
  −Task Week Ending Date

Figure 6.30   Output logical data accesses from the fourth decomposition.

After Adding Remaining Reports

The only change to the output logical data structures resulting from the decomposition and aggregation of the Monthly Task Report required data structure (Figure 6.11) is identification of Task Planned Date as a secondary key. The data relations remain unchanged; however, Task has a new data access for Task Planned Date.

The only change resulting from decomposition and aggregation of the Section Task Report required data structure (Figure 6.13) is addition of Task Hours Estimated to the Task entity. The data relations are not changed; however, a new access is added to Task consisting of Section Number and Task Number. A new access, consisting of Task Number only, is also added to Task Week.

Decomposition and addition of the Requester Task Report required data structure (Figure 6.15) and the Staff Task Report required data structure (Figure 6.17) do not change the output logical data structures or data relations. Two new accesses are added to Task, consisting of Requester Name and Task Number, and Staff SSN and Task Number. Figure 6.31 shows the output logical data structures after decomposition and aggregation of these four required data structures.

The output logical data relations are the same as those shown in Figure 6.27. The output logical data accesses are shown in Figure 6.32. The four new accesses for Task and the one new access for Task Week have been added.

Decomposition and aggregation of the Task Priority Report required data structure (Figure 6.19) adds a new entity for Code Table A to the output logical data structures. This Code Table A entity contains a primary key for Task Priority Code and an attribute for Task Priority Description.

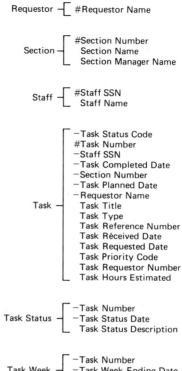

Requestor ⎯⎡ #Requestor Name

Section ⎯⎡ #Section Number
           │ Section Name
           ⎣ Section Manager Name

Staff ⎯⎡ #Staff SSN
       ⎣ Staff Name

Task ⎯⎡ −Task Status Code
      │ #Task Number
      │ −Staff SSN
      │ −Task Completed Date
      │ −Section Number
      │ −Task Planned Date
      │ −Requestor Name
      │ Task Title
      │ Task Type
      │ Task Reference Number
      │ Task Rèceived Date
      │ Task Requested Date
      │ Task Priority Code
      │ Task Requestor Number
      ⎣ Task Hours Estimated

Task Status ⎯⎡ −Task Number
             │ −Task Status Date
             ⎣ Task Status Description

Figure 6.31 Output logical data structures from the fifth decomposition.

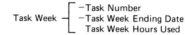

Task Week ⎯⎡ −Task Number
            │ −Task Week Ending Date
            ⎣ Task Week Hours Used

Final Output Data Entity Model

The final output logical data structures are shown in Figure 6.33. There are seven entities, with each entity containing one or more attributes that describe the entity.

The final output logical data relations are shown in Figure 6.34. Code Table A has been added with Task as a subordinate entity. Code Table A is also subordinate to Company.

The final output logical data accesses are shown in Figure 6.35. A new access has been added to Task for selecting and sequencing data. Code Table A has been added with its primary key.

The output data relation chart is shown in Figure 6.36. It is developed from the final output logical data relations shown in Figure 6.34.

The entities shown in the output data entity model are the data storages that will appear on the data flowcharts. These data storages supply data to

Requestor
  #Requestor Number

Section
  #Section Number

Staff
  #Staff SSN

Task
  −Task Status Code
  #Task Number

  −Staff SSN

  −Section Number
  −Task Status Code
  −Task Completed Date

  −Task Planned Date

  −Section Number
  #Task Number

  −Requestor Name
  #Task Number

  −Staff SSN
  #Task Number

Task Status
  −Task Number
  −Task Status Date

Task Week
  −Task Number
  −Task Week Ending Date
  −Task Number

Figure 6.32 Output logical data accesses from the fifth decomposition.

the processes that produce the outputs. All data required for the outputs are contained in these data storages.

DATA FLOWCHARTS

The data flowcharts for the Task Management System are developed in conjunction with the output definitions. As the outputs are defined and the required data structures decomposed, the logical data storages are identified. These logical data storages are placed on the data flowchart, with data flows to the processes producing the outputs.

The data flowchart for the three weekly task management reports that list only open and new tasks is shown in Figure 6.37. These reports require data from the data storages as identified on their respective required data structures. These requirements are indicated by the data flows from the data storages.

The Requester data storage is not shown on the data flowchart because it is not used. It contained only one attribute (Requester Name), which is the primary key and is also the foreign key in Task. Since the attribute is already

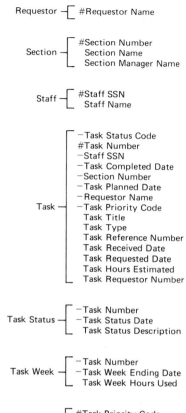

Requestor ⌐ #Requestor Name

Section ⌐ #Section Number
         ⎨ Section Name
         ⌐ Section Manager Name

Staff ⌐ #Staff SSN
      ⎩ Staff Name

Task ⌐ −Task Status Code
     ⎨ #Task Number
     ⎨ −Staff SSN
     ⎨ −Task Completed Date
     ⎨ −Section Number
     ⎨ −Task Planned Date
     ⎨ −Requestor Name
     ⎨ −Task Priority Code
     ⎨ Task Title
     ⎨ Task Type
     ⎨ Task Reference Number
     ⎨ Task Received Date
     ⎨ Task Requested Date
     ⎨ Task Hours Estimated
     ⎩ Task Requestor Number

Task Status ⌐ −Task Number
            ⎨ −Task Status Date
            ⎩ Task Status Description

Task Week ⌐ −Task Number
          ⎨ −Task Week Ending Date
          ⎩ Task Week Hours Used

Figure 6.33 Final output logical data structures for task management.

Code Table A ⌐ #Task Priority Code
             ⎩ Task Priority Description

Company
    Requestor
    Section
    Staff
    Code Table A
Requestor
    Task
Section
    Task
Staff
    Task
Task
    Task Status
    Task Week
Code Table A
    Task

Figure 6.34 Final output logical data relations for task management.

Requestor
  #Requestor Number

Section
  #Section Number

Staff
  #Staff SSN

Task
  −Task Status Code
  #Task Number

  −Staff SSN

  −Section Number
  −Task Status Code
  −Task Completed Date

  −Task Planned Date

  −Section Number
  #Task Number

  −Requestor Name
  #Task Number

  −Staff SSN
  #Task Number

  −Task Priority Code
  −Task Planned Date
  −Task Status Code

Task Status
  −Task Number
  −Task Status Date

Task Week
  −Task Number
  −Task Week Ending Date

  −Task Number

Code Table A
  #Task Priority Code

Figure 6.35   Final output logical data accesses for task management.

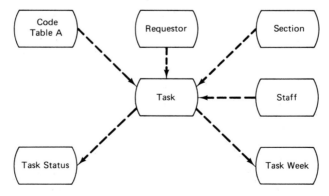

Figure 6.36   Output data relation chart for task management.

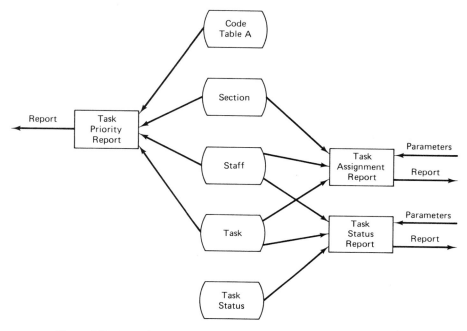

Figure 6.37 Data flowchart for weekly reports, listing open and new tasks.

available in the Task data storage, it is not necessary to obtain it from the Requester data storage.

Section and Staff data storages are accessed only for Section Name and Staff Name, respectively. There could be a tendency to place these names in the Task data storage to eliminate the accesses. However, this would not be consistent with a relational database design for two reasons.

First, it would create redundant data; i.e., both Section Name and Staff Name would be repeated once for each task and not once for their respective entities. This would cause update problems if any staff or section name were changed.

Second, in a company-wide database environment there is, or could be, other attributes for Section and Staff that are not used for task management. These attributes would be placed in the Section and Staff data storages. This keeps all attributes for each entity in a single data storage.

The data flowchart for the three weekly task management reports that list all tasks is shown in Figure 6.38. This information was obtained from the required data structures for each report the same as the data flowchart above.

The data flowchart for the three remaining task management reports is shown in Figure 6.39. Like the previous two data flowcharts, the information was obtained from the required data structures for the three reports.

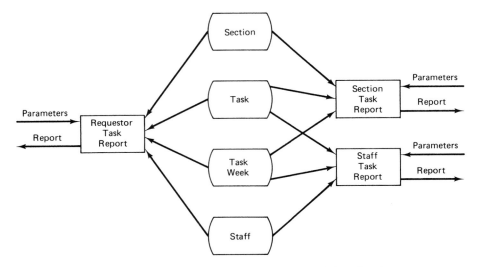

Figure 6.38 Data flowchart for weekly reports listing all tasks.

These three data flowcharts can be combined into one data flowchart for all task management outputs as shown in Figure 6.40. Each of the three previous data flowcharts is shown as a process on this combined data flowchart. All data storages needed for task management outputs are shown on this data flowchart.

Since these data storages provide data for task management outputs, they must be maintained by either task management inputs or some other input process. The Code Table A data storage is maintained by another process

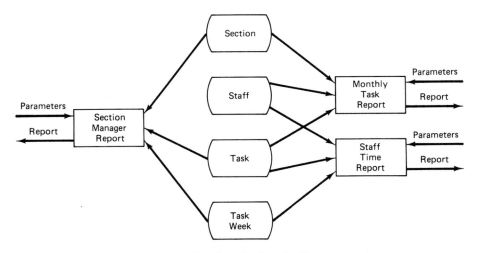

Figure 6.39 Data flowchart for the miscellaneous reports.

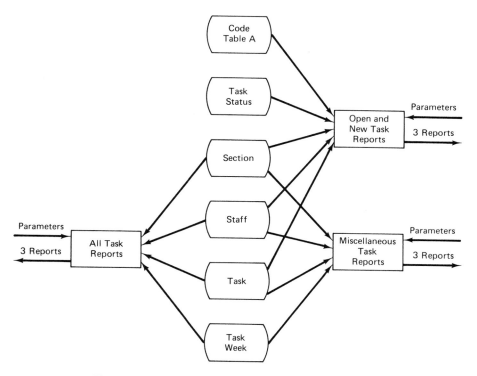

Figure 6.40 Data flowchart for all task management outputs.

and is not of concern to task management design. All other data storages must be maintained by task management inputs.

Four inputs are tentatively defined to maintain the five task management data storages. These inputs are shown on the data flowchart in Figure 6.41. Collectively, they must maintain all attributes in the task management data storages.

These inputs are tentative because it is not known if they will maintain all attributes. Each input must be defined with input and necessary data structures. The necessary data structures will then be decomposed to verify that all attributes are maintained.

INPUT DEFINITION

Input definition is very similar to output definition. An input data structure is developed for each input which shows the structure of the data on the input document. A necessary data structure is developed for each input which shows the structure of the data that maintains the data storages.

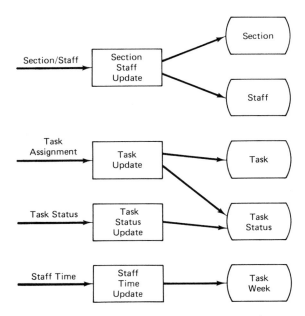

Figure 6.41   Data flowchart for task management inputs.

When the task management business activities and their inputs have been identified, these inputs can be defined. The business activities are a change in task status, weekly staff time, a new request, and a change in personnel. An input will be defined for each of these activities, including the input and necessary data structures.

Task Assignment Document

The Task Assignment document is used to assign a task to a staff person. When a request is received, one or more tasks are created. Each of these tasks is assigned to a staff person for completion.

The Task Assignment input data structure is shown in Figure 6.42. It shows all attributes on the Task Assignment document. The attributes identified by a left caret are not entered.

The Task Assignment necessary data structure is shown in Figure 6.43. Task Number is identified as a primary key which makes a task unique. If that task number already exists, a different task number will need to be assigned.

Requester Name, Section Number, and Staff SSN were identified in the output logical data structures as foreign keys in the Task Entity. These attributes must have values when a new task assignment is made.

Requester Name and Staff SSN are obtained from the input document.

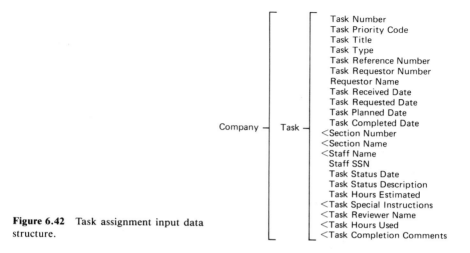

Figure 6.42 Task assignment input data structure.

Even though Section Number is on the input document, it may not be correct. Section Number is obtained from the staff entity based on Staff SSN.

Task is subordinate to Staff. Staff SSN is used to access the Staff entity to obtain Section Number, which is a foreign key in the Staff entity. Section Number is then placed in the Task entity as a derived attribute.

The Task Status entity is subordinate to the Task entity. Task Number is the secondary key in Task Status to identify the parent Task. Task Status Date and Task Status Description are entered in the Task Status entity.

The process logic for this document will be task driven. For each new

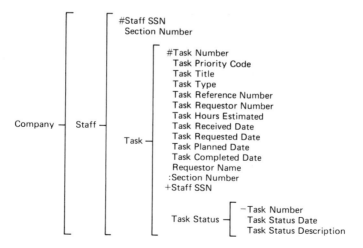

Figure 6.43 Task assignment necessary data structure.

task, a Task occurrence and a Task Status occurrence will be created. Staff will be accessed for Staff SSN.

Task Status Update Document

The Task Status Update document is used to add a task status description at any time during the duration of the task. Whenever the status of a task changes, or when a routine task status is due, a task status entry is made.

The Task Status Update input data structure is shown in Figure 6.44. Task Status Date and Task Status Description are always entered. Task Status Code is entered only if there is a change in the task status. The Task Reviewer Name is not entered.

The Task Status Update necessary data structure is shown in Figure 6.45. Task Status is shown subordinate to Task. Task Number is a foreign key in Task Status for identifying the parent Task.

The process logic for this document will be task-status driven. Each time a new task status is entered, a new task status occurrence is created. No check is made for other task status occurrences. Task is accessed if the Task Status Code needs to be changed.

Staff Time Update Document

The Staff Time Update document is used to enter each staff person's weekly time for each task he or she worked on during the week. These times are entered once each week.

The Staff Time Update input data structure is shown in Figure 6.46. Each Calendar Week a time sheet is received from each staff person. Calendar Week Ending Date is entered but is not placed on the database. Staff SSN, Staff Name, and Task Title are not entered.

The Staff Time Update necessary data structure is shown in Figure 6.47. Both Task Number and Task Week Ending Date are identified as primary keys

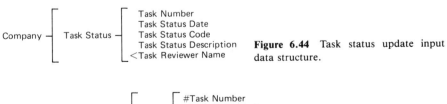

Figure 6.44 Task status update input data structure.

Figure 6.45 Task status update necessary data structure.

Figure 6.46   Staff time update input data structure.

Figure 6.47   Staff time update necessary
data structure.

Company — Task Week —
- #Task Number
- #Task Week Ending Date
- Task Week Hours Used

to assure that there is only one entry per task per week. Task Week Ending Date is obtained from Calendar Week Ending Date.

The process logic for this document is task-week driven. For each task week update, a check is made to determine if that occurrence already exists. If not, then it is added as a new occurrence.

Section Update Document

The Section Update document is used to update either section or staff data. The Section Update document shows the section name, number, manager name, and an update code. It also shows staff SSN, name, and an update code.

The Section Update input data structure is shown in Figure 6.48. The two update codes are entered but do not go to the database. The other attributes are updated depending on the update code.

The Section Update necessary data structure is shown in Figure 6.49.

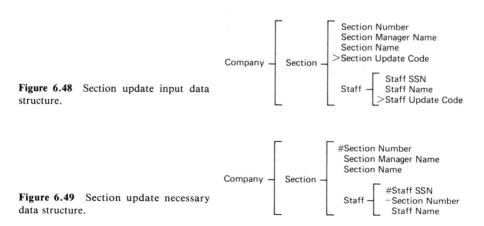

Figure 6.48   Section update input data
structure.

Figure 6.49   Section update necessary
data structure.

Staff is subordinate to Section. Section Number and Staff SSN are the primary keys for their respective entities.

If there are updates to the Section entity, it is accessed by Section Number. If there are updates to the Staff entity, it is accessed by Staff SSN. A section cannot be deleted if there are still staff assigned to it, and staff cannot be assigned to a section unless it is established.

The process logic for this document will be update driven. If a section is added, a new occurrence will be placed in the section entity. If a section is deleted, a check will be made for existing staff assigned to that section.

If a staff person is added, a check will be made to determine if the section exists. If it does, a new occurrence will be entered in the staff entity. A staff person cannot be deleted because of the historical tie to tasks.

These inputs should maintain all the attributes defined in the output data entity model. The input data entity model will determine if all attributes are maintained. If not, adjustments need to be made either to these inputs or to the outputs.

INPUT DATA ENTITY MODEL

The input data entity model is developed from the necessary data structures. Each necessary data structure is decomposed and the attributes are logically aggregated by entity. During decomposition the data relations and data accesses are recorded.

After Task Assignment Document

The Task Assignment necessary data structure (Figure 6.43) contains three entities: Staff, Task, and Task Status. The result of decomposition and aggregation of this data structure is shown in Figure 6.50.

The input logical data relations are shown in Figure 6.51. Staff is subordinate to Company, Task is subordinate to Staff, and Task Status is subordinate to Task.

The input logical data accesses are shown in Figure 6.52. Only one key is shown for each of the three entities.

Final Input Data Entity Model

The remaining three necessary data structures (Figures 6.45, 6.47, and 6.49) are decomposed and aggregated in a similar manner. The final input logical data structures are shown in Figure 6.53.

The final input logical data relations are shown in Figure 6.54. Task, Task Week, and Section have been added subordinate to Company. Section has been added with Staff as a subordinate.

The final input data accesses are shown in Figure 6.55. A second access

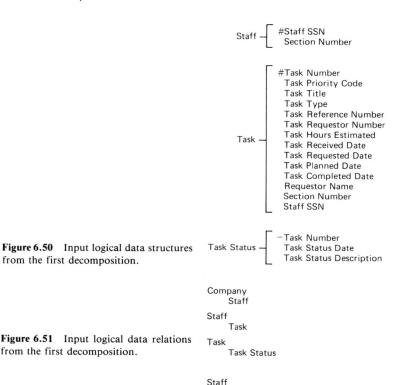

Staff ─┤ #Staff SSN
        Section Number

Task ─┤ #Task Number
        Task Priority Code
        Task Title
        Task Type
        Task Reference Number
        Task Requestor Number
        Task Hours Estimated
        Task Received Date
        Task Requested Date
        Task Planned Date
        Task Completed Date
        Requestor Name
        Section Number
        Staff SSN

Figure 6.50 Input logical data structures from the first decomposition.

Task Status ─┤ −Task Number
              Task Status Date
              Task Status Description

Company
   Staff

Staff
   Task

Task
   Task Status

Figure 6.51 Input logical data relations from the first decomposition.

Staff
   #Staff SSN

Task
   #Task Number

Task Status
   −Task Number

Figure 6.52 Input logical data accesses from the first decomposition.

has been added to Staff. Task Week has been added with two keys and Section has been added with one key.

The input data relation chart is shown in Figure 6.56. It is developed from the final input logical data relations shown in Figure 6.54.

The input data entity model should update all attributes in the database defined by the output data entity model. These two data models will be compared, and adjusted if necessary, to produce a total data entity model for task management.

TOTAL DATA ENTITY MODEL

The total data entity model is prepared by combining the input data entity model with the output data entity model. However, the two models must be compared first to identify any discrepancies. These discrepancies must be resolved or explained before the two models are combined.

```
              ┌ #Staff SSN
   Staff  ─┤    Section Number
              └ Staff Name

              ┌ #Task Number
                 Task Priority Code
                 Task Title
                 Task Type
                 Task Reference Number
                 Task Requestor Number
                 Task Hours Estimated
   Task   ─┤    Task Received Date
                 Task Requested Date
                 Task Planned Date
                 Task Completed Date
                 Requestor Name
                 Section Number
                 Staff SSN
              └ Task Status Code

                    ┌ #Task Number
   Task Status ─┤    Task Status Date
                    └ Task Status Description

                   ┌ #Task Number
   Task Week  ─┤    #Task Week Ending Date
                   └ Task Week Hours Used

                ┌ #Section Number
   Section  ─┤    Section Manager Name
                └ Section Name
```

Figure 6.53 Final input logical data structures for task management.

```
          Company
              Staff
              Task
              Task Week
              Section

          Staff
              Task

          Task
              Task Status

          Section
              Staff
```

Figure 6.54 Final input logical data relations for task management.

```
Staff
    #Staff SSN

    #Staff SSN
    −Section Number

Task
    #Task Number

Task Status
    −Task Number

Task Week
    #Task Number
    #Task Week Ending Date

Section
    #Section Number
```

Figure 6.55 Final input logical data accesses for task management.

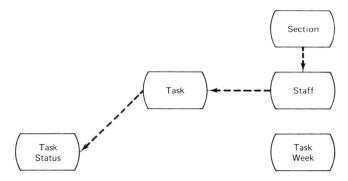

Figure 6.56   Input data relation chart for task management.

Logical Data Structures

The final output logical data structures are shown in Figure 6.33, and the final input logical data structures are shown in Figure 6.53. All entities and attributes shown on the input logical data structures are contained on the output logical data structures except Section Number within Staff. In addition, the output logical data structures contain Requester with one attribute and Code Table A with two attributes.

The addition of Section Number within Staff is reasonable because Staff is subordinate to Section, and Staff changes and Section changes could affect each other. The relation between Section and Staff did not appear in the outputs because no reports were identified for Staff by Section.

The Requester discrepancy is reasonable. The only attribute in Requester is Requester Name, which is also a foreign key in Task. Since it is unreasonable to use Requester Name to go to Requester to obtain Requester Name, the Requester entity will not be used in Task Management. This is verified by a lack of Requester on the input logical data structures.

The Code Table A discrepancy is also reasonable. As was mentioned earlier, Code Table A was maintained by another process outside of task management. Therefore, it would not appear on the input logical data structures.

The three discrepancies have been explained. If they could not be explained, an adjustment would have to be made to the inputs, the outputs, or both, until the discrepancies are resolved.

The input and output logical data structures can now be combined. The total logical data structures for task management are shown in Figure 6.57. These structures will be used to define the database model.

The Requester entity is included in the data structures because it may be used in other systems or at a later date. Even though it is not used in task management, it cannot be deleted from the logical database. The reference to Requester must be carried to the company total logical database.

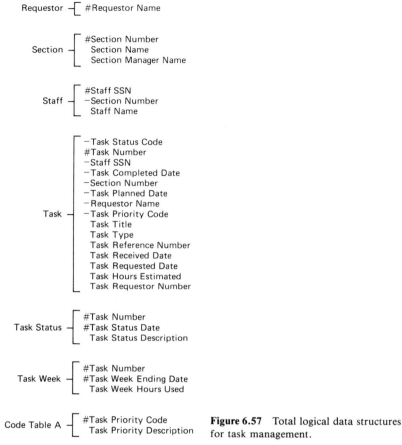

Requestor ─[#Requestor Name

Section ─[#Section Number
            Section Name
            Section Manager Name

Staff ─[#Staff SSN
         −Section Number
         Staff Name

Task ─[−Task Status Code
        #Task Number
        −Staff SSN
        −Task Completed Date
        −Section Number
        −Task Planned Date
        −Requestor Name
        −Task Priority Code
        Task Title
        Task Type
        Task Reference Number
        Task Received Date
        Task Requested Date
        Task Hours Estimated
        Task Requestor Number

Task Status ─[#Task Number
               #Task Status Date
               Task Status Description

Task Week ─[#Task Number
             #Task Week Ending Date
             Task Week Hours Used

Code Table A ─[#Task Priority Code
                Task Priority Description

Figure 6.57   Total logical data structures for task management.

Code Table A is included in the data structures because it is used by task management. When task management logical data structures are merged with the company total logical data structures, Code Table A appears as part of the Code Tables used by the company. This provides a reference to all uses of each code table.

Logical Data Relations

The combined logical data relations for task management are shown in Figure 6.58. The final output logical data relations in Figure 6.34 and the final input logical data relations in Figure 6.54 were added to produce the combined data relations. These data relations will be used with the combined data accesses to define the database model.

Company
    Requestor
    Section
    Staff
    Code Table A
    Task Week
    Task

Requestor
    Task

Section
    Task
    Staff

Staff
    Task

Task
    Task Status
    Task Week

Code Table A
    Task

Figure 6.58 Total logical data relations for task management.

Logical Data Accesses

The combined logical data accesses for task management are shown in Figure 6.59. The final output logical data accesses in Figure 6.35 and the final input logical data accesses in Figure 6.55 were added to produce the combined data accesses. These data accesses will be used to develop the database model.

Data Relation Chart

The total data relation chart for task management is shown in Figure 6.60. It can be developed from the total logical data relations in Figure 6.58, or from a combination of the output data relation chart in Figure 6.36 and the input data relation chart in Figure 6.56. Either way is acceptable and both could be done for verification.

Data Flowchart

The final data flowchart for the task management inputs is shown in Figure 6.61. It is basically the same as the initial input data flowchart shown in Figure 6.41. However, there are several additions.

The Section Staff Update process must access both Section and Staff data storages to determine if sections can be deleted and staff can be added. These additions are shown by a double data flow between the update process and the Section and Staff data storages.

The Task Update process must access the Staff data storage to obtain the section number. Therefore, a data flow is added from the Staff data storage to the Task Update process.

Requestor
    #Requestor Name

Section
    #Section Number

Staff
    #Staff SSN

    #Staff SSN
    −Section Number

Task
    #Task Status Code
    #Task Number

    −Staff SSN

    −Section Number
    −Task Status Code
    −Task Completed Date

    −Task Planned Date

    −Section Number
    #Task Number

    −Requestor Name
    #Task Number

    −Staff SSN
    #Task Number

    −Task Priority Code
    −Task Planned Date
    −Task Status Code

    #Task Number

Task Status
    −Task Number
    −Task Status Date

    #Task Number

Task Week
    #Task Number
    #Task Week Ending Date

    −Task Number

Code Table A
    #Task Priority Code

Figure 6.59   Total logical data accesses for task management.

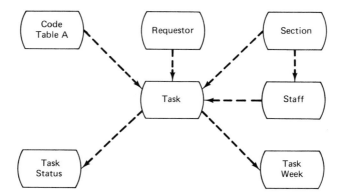

Figure 6.60   Total data relation chart for task management.

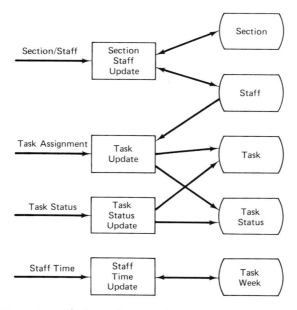

Figure 6.61   Final data flowchart for task management inputs.

A data flow is also added from the Task Status Update process to the Task data storage. This data flow is necessary to update the Task Status Code.

The last addition is a double data flow between the Staff Time Update process and the Task Week data storage. The Task Week data storage must be accessed to determine if the week to be added already exists. If not, it will be added.

These changes could not have been reasonably predicted when the tentative input data flowchart was developed. However, when the necessary data structures were developed, it became obvious that additional data flows were needed. When the input and output data entity models were finalized and combined, the new data flows were added to the input data flowchart.

Business Information Model

The business information model for task management is shown in Figure 6.62. It is actually a portion of the total business information model for the entire company. However, only the task management portion is shown for clarity.

This portion of the business information model shows that task management has four input documents and nine reports. Five data storages are accessed and updated and one data storage is accessed only. When this model is added to the total company model, there will be an update process for Code Table A, and there could be accesses to the other data storages.

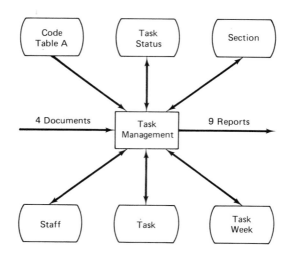

Figure 6.62 Business information model for task management.

The total data entity model is used to develop the database model. All the logical pieces have been defined to meet the requirements of the system. They can be manipulated to produce a database model that is optimum for the operating environment and still meet the needs of task management.

The data flowcharts will be used to develop the process logic. Each process will be defined in detail and instructions will be developed. The appropriate physical files will be accessed to obtain or update the data.

PHYSICAL DATABASE

The database model is developed from the data entity model according to the specific operating environment. The physical data files are then implemented into that operating environment according to the database model. The applications access the physical data files according to the database model.

It is not the intent of this book to explain the development of database models in detail. There are just too many different operating environments and too many database management systems. However, a brief example of possible task management database models will illustrate how a database model is produced.

One option for task management is to make the database model identical to the data entity model. There would be six physical files, one for each entity on the data entity model. There would be a data item in each file for each attribute in the corresponding entity.

The physical data structures would look just like the logical data structures in Figure 6.57, minus the Requester entity. Requester, as mentioned earlier, is not used. Physical keys would be identified exactly as shown in the logical data accesses.

If super-keys were used, they would be developed according to the data accesses shown in Figure 6.59, minus the Requester entity. The Task physical data structure, with super-keys, is shown in Figure 6.63. Each data access becomes a super-key with the attributes themselves listed below the keys.

The physical data accesses would be the same as the logical data accesses shown in Figure 6.59. The database chart is shown in Figure 6.64. The accesses match the data relations shown in Figure 6.60 because there are no many-to-many relations.

If a hierarchical database management system is used, the required and necessary data structures indicate the hierarchies that are developed. These data structures show the data accesses and the attributes that are obtained on each access.

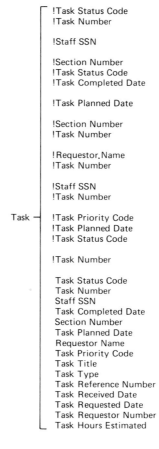

Figure 6.63 Task physical data structure with super-keys for task management.

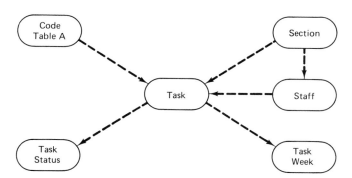

Figure 6.64 Database chart for task management.

Another option for a task management database model is to combine Task Week and Task Status with Task. Task is the only parent to these two entities and it is unlikely there will be other parents. Each of these two entities would be repeating entities within Task.

The physical data structure for this option is shown in Figure 6.65. Task Status and Task Week are shown within Task. Each still contains its respective attributes. Task Number has been removed from Task Week and Task Status. Since Task Number is used to obtain the Task occurrence, it is not needed to obtain any repeating entity within that Task occurrence.

Task Week and Task Status could be multiple record types within Task. The physical data structure for this option is shown in Figure 6.66. Task Description is added as the set label for the attributes describing each Task.

Task Record Type has been added as an attribute to define the record type. Task Number remains as a key to both Task Status and Task Week.

The database chart for these two options is shown in Figure 6.67. Task Status and Task Week do not show on the chart since they are internal to Task. The physical data structure identifies where these two entities are located.

These brief examples have shown how the database model is developed from the data entity model. There are many alternatives to evaluate and many options for developing the database model. When the model is completed, the physical files can be implemented and the process logic for accessing those files can be developed.

PROCESS LOGIC

Process logic is developed for each process on the data flowcharts. This process logic manipulates the incoming data flows to produce the outgoing data flows. With automated processes the data flows may involve the physical data files.

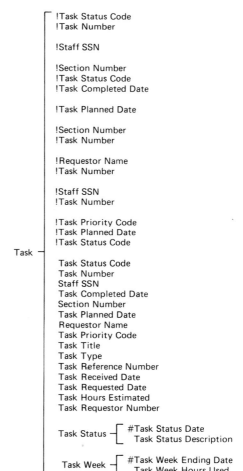

!Task Status Code
!Task Number

!Staff SSN

!Section Number
!Task Status Code
!Task Completed Date

!Task Planned Date

!Section Number
!Task Number

!Requestor Name
!Task Number

!Staff SSN
!Task Number

!Task Priority Code
!Task Planned Date
!Task Status Code

Task

Task Status Code
Task Number
Staff SSN
Task Completed Date
Section Number
Task Planned Date
Requestor Name
Task Priority Code
Task Title
Task Type
Task Reference Number
Task Received Date
Task Requested Date
Task Hours Estimated
Task Requestor Number

Task Status ⎯ ⎡ #Task Status Date
                ⎣ Task Status Description

Task Week ⎯ ⎡ #Task Week Ending Date
              ⎣ Task Week Hours Used

Figure 6.65 Physical data structure for task management with repeating groups.

It is not the intent of this book to provide a detailed explanation of process logic, or to provide examples of source code. There are just too many operating environments, and they are so varied that they could form a book of their own. However, a brief example for task management is presented to illustrate how process logic is developed.

In this example, two generic terms will be used to prevent association with any specific operating environment. *Acquire* means to obtain data from the physical file. *Deposit* means to place data into the physical file.

The exact mechanism for acquiring and depositing data depends on the specific operating environment and a company's standards. It is not important in this process logic. What is important is how the process logic is developed and when the physical files are accessed.

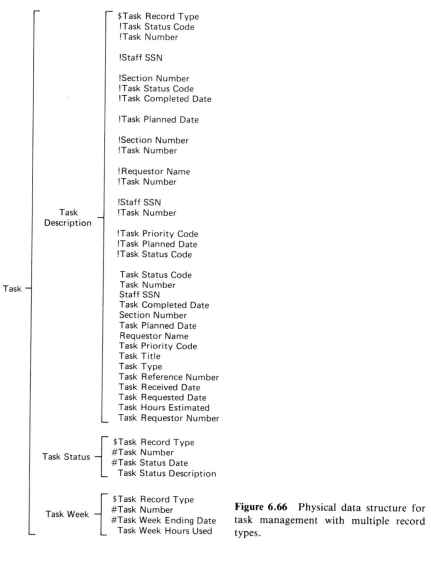

Task — Task Description:

```
$Task Record Type
!Task Status Code
!Task Number

!Staff SSN

!Section Number
!Task Status Code
!Task Completed Date

!Task Planned Date

!Section Number
!Task Number

!Requestor Name
!Task Number

!Staff SSN
!Task Number

!Task Priority Code
!Task Planned Date
!Task Status Code

Task Status Code
Task Number
Staff SSN
Task Completed Date
Section Number
Task Planned Date
Requestor Name
Task Priority Code
Task Title
Task Type
Task Reference Number
Task Received Date
Task Requested Date
Task Hours Estimated
Task Requestor Number
```

Task Status:

```
$Task Record Type
#Task Number
#Task Status Date
Task Status Description
```

Task Week:

```
$Task Record Type
#Task Number
#Task Week Ending Date
Task Week Hours Used
```

Figure 6.66 Physical data structure for task management with multiple record types.

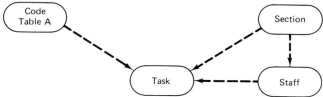

Figure 6.67 Database chart for task management with repeating entities or multiple record types.

Task Status Report

The output data structure for the Task Status report is shown in Figure 6.4. This data structure is the basic structure of the process logic. The logic operations will be placed in this structure to obtain the data and print the report.

The required data structure for the Task Status report is shown in Figure 6.5. This data structure shows the data items that are acquired from each of the physical files. These are the logical views of data needed from the database to produce the report.

The process logic for the Task Status report is shown in Figure 6.68. Company is the highest level because the report is produced for the company. Each Task is a repetitive set within Company for listing open and new tasks. Each Task Status is a repetitive set within Task for listing the status descriptions.

The Begin Company set acquires the Run Date, prints title, headings, and Run Date, and clears the Staff Name. The first open or new task is acquired in Begin Company. This will be the open or new task with the lowest Task Number.

The Begin Task set checks to see if the staff person from the preceding task is the same as the staff person for the current task. If not, the Staff Name is acquired from the Staff file. The task data is then printed. The first task status description for the task is acquired in Begin Task.

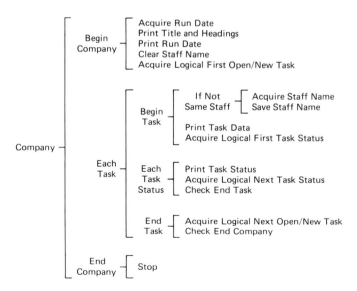

Figure 6.68 Process logic for task status report.

The Each Task Status set prints the task status description and acquires the next task status for the task. A check is made to determine if there is a task status or if the end of the task has been reached. If there are more status descriptions for the task, Each Task Status set is repeated.

The End Task set acquires the next open or new task. A check is made to determine if there is another task or if the end of the company has been reached. If there are more tasks, the Each Task set is repeated.

Another example of process logic for the Task Status report is shown in Figure 6.69. The structure of the process logic is the same as Figure 6.68. Only the method of acquiring data is different.

The number and sequence of all open and new tasks is determined in the Begin Company set. The Each Task set is then repeated for each task found. No checks are made for end of company.

The number and sequence of all task status descriptions are determined in the Begin Task set. The Each Task Status set is then repeated for each task status found. No checks are made for end of task.

The database model is consulted to determine the physical storage for these files. In the earlier section on physical database, three options were shown for storing task status records: a separate data file, a repeating entity within task, and a multiple record type. The keys used will vary depending on which physical data file option was used.

For instance, if a separate data file were used for Task Status, the key would be Task Number and Task Status Date. If Task Status were a repeating

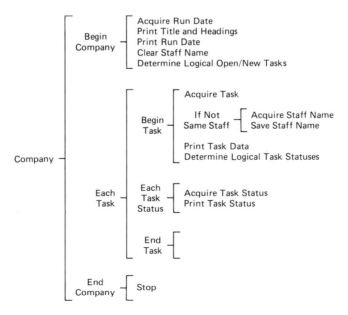

Figure 6.69 Process logic for task status report.

group within Task, only Task Status Date would be used. If Task Status were a multiple record type within Task, the key would be Task Record Type, Task Number, and Task Status Date.

Task Status Update

The input data structure for Task Status Update is shown in Figure 6.44, and the necessary data structure is shown in Figure 6.45. This update process will be driven by incoming task status descriptions. Task Status will be updated and Task could be updated.

The process logic for the Task Status Update is shown in Figure 6.70. The first Task Status is read in the Begin Company set. All other task statuses are read in the End Task Status set.

If there is a change in Task Status Code, the Task occurrence is acquired, changed, and deposited in the alternative set. The task status descriptions are deposited in the End Task Status set. When the end of data is reached, processing stops.

These process logic examples have been simple, but they illustrate how physical files are accessed. The principles of data-structured process logic apply whether the logic is simple or detailed, whether it is on-line or batch, and whether a database management system or conventional files are used. Only the details change based on the operating environment.

SUMMARY

The task management case study has illustrated how the data-structured database design method is used to design and develop a database. The example

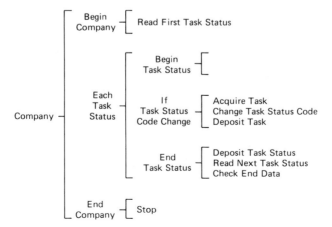

Figure 6.70   Process logic for task status update.

has been brief and simple compared to most systems developed today. However, it covered all steps of database design and most of the situations encountered in database design.

The design process began with a description of the environment and development of a business entity model. Data flowcharts were defined, including output and required data structures. Based on the required data structures, an output data entity model was developed.

A tentative data flowchart was developed for inputs, and inputs were defined with input and necessary data structures. An input data entity model was developed and compared to the output data entity model. Any discrepancies were explained or resolved, and a total data entity model was developed.

The data flowcharts were adjusted based on the data entity model and a business information model was developed. The database model was developed from the data entity model. The physical files would be implemented depending on the specific operating environment.

Process logic would be developed for each process on the data flowchart. This process logic would access the physical files to obtain or update data to meet the user needs. The specific process logic depends on the particular operating environment.

Several pitfalls await the unwary database designer. The data structures must be developed only for the specific input or output they represent. No assumptions should be made about future use or other inputs and outputs.

Each data structure must be unique to the input or output it represents to maintain control of database design. As systems are developed and modified, inputs and outputs are included and excluded. If data structures do not represent just their input or output, the wrong database could be generated.

When there are only a few attributes in an entity, there is a strong tendency to store them in another entity where they are used. This appears to save time accessing another data file to obtain one or two data items. However, it defeats the purpose of subject databases.

Storing data according to how it is used by an application is reverting to the traditional application file concept. In the company-wide database environment, data must be stored by subject entity. This concept provides maximum productivity for the company.

There can be confusion about the priority, or importance, of keys. A primary key indicates uniqueness and access. Once an attribute is identified as a primary key in the data entity model, it cannot be reduced to a secondary or foreign key.

A secondary key indicates access only and does not indicate any uniqueness. It is used to identify an access path into an entity. It is less important than a primary key.

A foreign key indicates an attribute used to access a foreign entity. It is not an access path into the entity where it is stored. It is less important than a secondary key.

The worst pitfall is to predict the physical data files without any analysis or design. This will inevitably lead to the wrong data files with the wrong attributes. For instance, Figure 6.71 shows the original task management database requested by the designer in charge of the task management project.

Several major discrepancies are obvious when this data structure is compared to the database model. First, there are three files, for Manager, Task, and Employee. The database model showed six files, for Section, Staff (Employee), Task, Task Week, Task Status, and Code Table A.

Second, the attributes are not named consistently. The names do not begin with the entity name, even assuming that they were in the correct entity. Many of the names are incomplete or not fully descriptive.

Third, there are many attributes shown as stored on the database that are neither used nor updated. There are also attributes, according to the data-

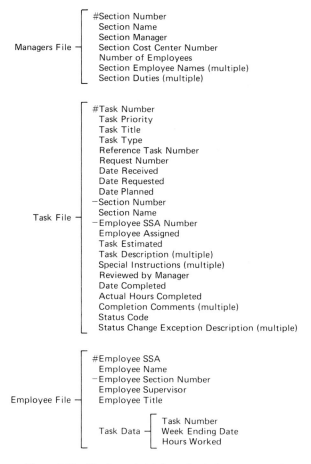

Figure 6.71   Unplanned database for task management.

base model, that are used and updated that do not appear. These two situations will result in an inefficient database that will not meet the user requirements.

Fourth, the keys identified will not meet the input or output requirements. There is no way all the inputs could be processed or the outputs produced with the keys that are identified.

There are other problems of lesser importance. The point to be made is that a "brute force" physical file development without a formal design will result in an inefficient, ineffective database. The only way to assure an effective, efficient database is with a formal database design method.

The data-structured database design method provides a formal design method that produces effective, efficient databases. It provides a logical design based on user requirements followed by a physical implementation into a specific operating environment. It improves the productivity of people and increases the chances for a company to survive in a dynamic business environment.

STUDY QUESTIONS

1. What operating environmental characteristics are considered for developing the database model?
2. What options are available for developing the database model?
3. What are the disadvantages of a direct physical file design?
4. How are business entity models kept simple?
5. What is the priority or importance of keys?
6. What is the difference between output data structures and required data structures?
7. Why is an entity included in the total data entity model if it is not used by the application?
8. What are some alternatives that could be used in task management design?
9. What are the pitfalls in database design, and how can they be avoided?
10. How is process logic developed for accessing the database?

7

MANAGING INFORMATION

Knowledge is power. Those that have the knowledge have the power to control their destiny. Companies that have the knowledge have the power to control their survival in the business environment.

Knowledge is the awareness, and understanding, of information. It is the accumulation of, and acquaintance with, a large set of facts. For a company these facts pertain, directly or indirectly, to the business environment in which the company is competing.

The chances for survival, and success, of a company depend on the accumulated information it has available. Better information means a better chance for success. Better information means the right information, at the right time, in the right place. The right information means accurate, appropriate facts in the proper form.

When companies can have good, accurate facts in the right form, when they need them, where they need them, better decisions can be made. Better decisions assure that company goals can be achieved. When goals are achieved, a company is successful.

A business revolution is in progress where companies are following better business practices. These better practices demand better information. As business practices get better and the business environment gets more dynamic, the demand for information grows.

The growing demand for better information, plus faster, less expensive information-processing hardware, has resulted in an information explosion. More and more data are available to the user. However, so many individual facts are now available that people are reaching a data overload.

This data overload is due largely to poorly conceived and poorly designed information systems. These systems are producing too many facts in the wrong form, at the wrong time, in the wrong place. This is precisely what is not needed for a company to be successful.

A company needs less data and more information to manage its business affairs. Information systems need to process and summarize more data into information, present that information in a better form, and even begin to make business decisions based on that information.

The development of large batch or on-line, event-driven systems built solely by data-processing professionals takes too long and does not meet user needs. This approach should be used only for the large backbone systems in a company. Support systems, including ad hoc capability, should be developed for the more dynamic information needs.

End users, from administrator to technician, must be directly involved in the design of information systems. They must have direct interface to the data they need to perform their duties. This interface can be on-line systems, batch reports, ad hoc capabilities, or an information center.

Regardless of what information is needed to manage a company, the basic data must be captured, edited, stored, accessed, maintained, and destroyed. This process requires a well-planned, well-designed, well-developed database. Without that database the best intentions will result in business failure.

INFORMATION RESOURCE MANAGEMENT

End users must have a direct interface to the data and information they need to perform their business duties. This interface may be batch processing, on-line conversations, ad hoc inquiry, information centers, or any number of other possibilities. The method is not necessarily important as long as users can obtain the data they need, when they need it.

This need has led to a business-driven information strategy. Data is viewed as a corporate asset and is managed in the same way as any other resource. Integrated databases are developed that are shared, with proper authorization, by many users.

Good business planning must include information planning. Business planners must know and understand the need for information planning. Information planners must know and understand the business and its information needs. Information must be planned for and managed to meet the business needs.

The system design issues of today will become the data design issues of tomorrow. Application-oriented systems are evolving into data-oriented systems. Record-keeping functions are evolving into decision support functions and knowledge-based functions.

Information resource management is emerging as a formal discipline for managing data to produce information that can be retained as knowledge to support the business. Its objective is to get the right data to the right people at the right time in the right form. It is a discipline to manage a rapidly changing, highly dynamic technology to provide information support for better business management.

Information resource management is the management of data to produce information that can be retained as knowledge. It is based on the concept that data is a corporate asset that should be managed like any other asset. Information, second only to people, is a company's most valuable asset, and may well be listed on the company's financial report.

Information resource management pertains to data the same as human resource management pertains to people. Data, like people, are subject to sound management principles. They are subject to organization, planning, control, inventory, cost accounting, and budgeting.

Information resource management emphasizes a shift from the management of people and their computers to the management of information as a resource to meet people's needs. To be successful, there must be better information system coordination and integration. There must be more information awareness and information sharing. Above all, there must be an improvement in productivity.

Information resource management requires a complete corporate information architecture. This architecture establishes the structure and definition of the company's data. It is this meta-data that defines attribute names, subject entities, and the logical data model for the company.

The trends in information, systems, source languages, and databases demand good, sound information resource management. They demand good, sound information engineering and software engineering principles. Without good management practices and good engineering principles the appropriate data will not be available to produce the information necessary to meet user needs.

MANAGEMENT STRATEGIES

Strategy is the science of planning and directing large-scale operations. It requires skill at developing a plan of action to achieve some end objective. It also requires knowledge and techniques to carry out these plans.

Information resource management in many companies is definitely a large-scale operation that requires good planning and good directing to be successful. This success depends on having good strategies for information resource management. These strategies must, of course, be consistent with the overall strategies of the company.

Management Commitment

Company management must be committed to, and involved in, proactive management of the information resource. Information is a vital resource that affects decisions, productivity, and profit. These, in turn, determine whether a company will survive or fail in a competitive business environment.

Managers must set the overall company needs and perspective, both long term and short term. They must set priorities based on these needs and establish plans for achieving goals. They must allocate budgets to carry out the plans.

Managers must also set the framework for company standards and encourage the development of, and adherence to, those standards. They must encourage productivity improvement by avoiding any uncoordinated, redundant development effort. They must minimize the impact of company politics on the achievement of productivity improvement.

Managers must be aware of information trends and the tools and techniques for information management. They must be aware that isolated, fragmented, user-developed systems must be maintained, usually by the professional data-processing staff. They must be aware that extensive analysis and reorganization of applications and data may lead to reorganization of the company.

Managers must be willing to understand the magnitude and benefits of a database environment. They must be willing to accept the investment in them and dollars to achieve that environment. Finally, they must make a sustained commitment to the success of that database environment.

Above all, managers must realize that they cannot abdicate responsibility or dictate directions. They must be committed to, and directly involved in, the direction of information management. Their commitment and involvement will assure the success of the company.

Information Planning

Following management commitment to a database environment, an information plan must be developed. That plan must be integrated with the company's total plan and must meet the goals and objectives of the company. A total plan, and management involvement in the development of that plan, are essential for a successful database environment.

Information planning has two aspects. First is planning at the company level for company-wide management of the information resource. Second, when the company-wide plan is completed, a detailed plan is prepared for the development, use, and maintenance of the database itself.

Management of information begins at the company level. There is a current trend from information system planning to business information planning oriented toward information needed to solve business problems. This business orientation identifies what information is needed, where it is needed, and when it is needed.

Both company managers and information system managers must be involved in the planning effort. Working-level users must also be involved in planning, or at least have representation in the planning effort. The plan must meet the needs of all users from top management to the working level.

If the information plan is a long-term plan, it is best to get started. A short-term information plan could afford a delayed implementation, but a long-term information plan must be implemented as soon as possible. Therefore, the longer it will take to have a database environment, the quicker the plan should be implemented.

Although this is not a text on developing an information plan, a few guidelines can be offered. These guidelines describe the concepts, principles, and standards that should be established when moving into a database environment. They also describe what could happen if these concepts, principles, and standards are not established.

Data should be recognized as a corporate asset that is managed in the same way as any other corporate asset. It should be stored with minimum redundancy and should be shared by all users with the appropriate authority. The data is not owned by a single user or single application.

One of the obstacles to company-owned data shared by all users is that users may not agree to share their data. This hesitation to share data is propagated by the availability of personal computers, where users can still retain their private data. Although this may be acceptable in some instances, data that is of use to more than one user must be shared by those users for a database environment to be successful.

The structure of the data must be kept separate from the structure of the applications. This concept of data independence assures that applications are structured according to the business activities they serve and that data is structured according to the subject it describes. This allows the structure of either one to change with minimum impact on the other.

A good database environment will maintain a balance between the structure of business applications, the structure of subject data, and the use of data by the applications. An overemphasis on business applications will lead to application-oriented data files. This leads to the traditional redundancy problems and related storage anomalies.

An over emphasis on data will lead to application inflexibility, and changes will be difficult. Data designers lose sight of the commonality of data between applications. They also lose sight of the goals and objectives of the business and are unable to communicate effectively with end users.

An overemphasis on the use of data provides abundant data to flexible applications but fails to set an information plan consistent with the company plan. While abundant data and flexible applications are desirable, both must follow a plan that is consistent with company goals and objectives. Therefore, there must be equal emphasis on planning business applications, subject data, and the use of data by the applications.

Database design must follow a formal method and the company must commit to that method. That method must emphasize logical design before physical implementation. It must include procedures to handle retrofits and interfaces to existing applications. It must be based on sound theory and be self-documenting. Above all, it must be easy to understand and use.

Design the database according to the current requirements, then modify the database as future requirements are identified. Do not attempt to predict all the future requirements for the database. Unforeseen details are missed, which could mean changing the database, which is usually more difficult than expanding the database.

However, do not use the lack of future detail as an excuse not to design a database for the current applications. Good logical design and physical implementation of a relational database allow the database to grow with the changing needs of the company.

A relational database gives the most flexible database for meeting changing application needs, yet the most stable database as far as one application's changes affecting other applications. This makes design easier because the database has no rigid, predetermined structure. Since design is easier, the planning for information systems is easier.

Business data becomes relatively stable with time. It is the subsets of the business data and the relations between those subsets that are dynamic. The relational model allows the subject data to become stable, yet allows great flexibility in defining new subsets of data and new relations between those subsets.

Database design should be based largely on backbone systems. This will identify most of the attributes in each subject entity and many of the relations. However, the design method should also allow for ad hoc applications, which usually add a few new attributes but identify many new subsets of data and many new relations.

The design method should not result in paralysis by analysis. There must be a thorough analysis of the data, but the analysis must be performed as quickly as possible and with minimum effort. Any unnecessary effort or delay results in a loss of productivity.

This is particularily true for ad hoc applications. The tendency is either to treat ad hoc requests as backbone applications and overanalyze the data requirements, or to ignore data analysis completely. Ad hoc requests must receive sufficient data analysis to assure that data is available and is retrieved in the most efficient manner, yet not enough analysis to paralyze the usefulness of the ad hoc request capability.

A sound database strategy should be established. Most certainly there should be a database management system, but not every data file belongs in the database management system. Specific criteria must be established for determining whether or not a data file should be in the database management system.

Once a database strategy is chosen, there should be commitment to that strategy. Switching database strategies can be a monumental task. Starting with the wrong strategy could mean starting over.

A database management system must be well-designed, based on a good logical design and a good specification of the operating environment. A poor database management system design will result in just another access method that could be very expensive. A good database management system design is a catalyst to use that system and to expand its use.

A database management system is not a cure-all for providing data to applications. A good database management system requires good planning and good design and an in-depth understanding of database technology. Implementation of a database management system should not be taken lightly or attempted by inexperienced people.

When planning for a database environment, it is important to remember that the process is an evolution, not a revolution. There is a shift from an application orientation to a data orientation, and from the management of applications to the management of data. This shift should be slow but steady to be successful.

During this shift, technical issues will arise that are certainly important, but are not critical. It is the people issues that arise that are critical to the success of a database environment. These people issues must be resolved constructively for a successful database environment.

One way to solve, and even prevent, serious people issues is the formulation of standards about the development and use of a database environment. Since these standards have an effect on the responsibilities of many people, those people should be involved in the preparation of standards. Well-planned, constructive, cooperative development of standards will assure success.

One major area that standards must address is the development of applications and databases. There must be some management control over what is developed and who does the development.

These controls cannot be so rigid as to prevent users from getting the information they need. Nor can they be so loose as to allow fragmentation and development of applications and data files that will never be compatible. There must be an appropriate mix of control for uniformity and information availability that meets the company's goals.

Problems will arise as evolution to a database environment progresses. These problems should be faced, analyzed, and solved. One way to assure failure is to avoid making important decisions that would resolve major problems.

When resolving problems, it is necessary to make sure that the basic problem has been identified. Too often, simple solutions are implemented for symptomatic problems. The basic problem still exists and will continue to surface until it is resolved.

When resolving problems, as well as establishing standards, all parties involved must be willing to compromise. Nothing invites failure as much as several groups in open conflict where neither group is willing to compromise. Actually, all parties lose because the company's goals are not met.

Failure can also occur by overstating potential savings or understating development time and costs. Unreasonable or irrelevant projects can also lead to failure. To avoid such situations, a formal plan must be developed and constantly revised as priorities change, as problems are encountered, and as new information is available.

Planning is vital to successful information management. It can resolve high backlogs, high maintenance, and user frustration by organizing and controlling the development and use of the information resource. Planning helps meet business goals and increases productivity.

Data Administration

The concept of data administration today is that all data in a company are managed as a corporate asset. Data have a cost to acquire, a cost to maintain, and in many cases a cost to destroy. Like other company assets, data can be inventoried, they have a useful life, and they can be evaluated by a benefit-cost analysis.

The effective management of the data resource begins with establishment of a formal data administration function. The administration of data is no different from the administration of funds, personnel, motor pools, or any other resource. Like these other resources, data must have a formal administration.

Evolution of the data administration function is similar to evolution of the public information officer. The public information officer was needed to control the release of secure and sensitive information to employees and to the public. The data administrator is needed to control the development and use of data within the company. The result of no data administration is the same chaotic situation that existed when there was no public information officer.

Administration of data must begin with a resource inventory. Inventory requires a good information resource directory which, in its simplest form, provides a list of data that exists in the company. This basic inventory may be revised and expanded as necessary to manage the company's data effectively.

Implementation of the data administration function leads to the question of ownership of data. It is the company that owns the data, and within that ownership there are responsibilities for managing that data. The end user manages the data that provides information for them to achieve their goals. Data administration manages the meta-data: the data about the data.

Administration of data must include a formal logical database design. That method must include the business environment as well as the data needed to operate in that environment. A method that considers only the data and not the business may well produce a logical database that does not meet the needs of the business.

A successful database design method must include data models. A really successful database design method must also include business models. When business models are developed about the business and data models are developed based on the business models, the data will meet the needs of the business.

Administration of data includes data security and integrity. The data must be kept secure from unauthorized access, alteration, and destruction. An authorization procedure must be established to control access and identify attempted breaches to that control.

The control of data access cuts across organizational boundaries. The best way to control access is for data administration to maintain the access control mechanism, while user management identifies the access authority for individual users. Whenever users control the access mechanism or data administration designates user access, authority problems will arise.

Availability of data means that data must be available when and where the user needs that data. Availability of data includes good backup and recovery after failures and disasters. Data administration must work closely with operations, users, and systems development personnel to prepare backup and recovery plans and procedures. The best of data is useless if it cannot be restored after a disaster.

Data administration must be directly involved in the movement, or transmission, of data and its security and integrity during transmission. As the use of communication networks, distributed data, and distributed processing expands, the function of data security and integrity also expands. Data security and integrity plans and backup and recovery plans must keep pace with the transmission of data.

As companies become more decentralized, the question of control becomes more important. There must be central management control of the data resource to prevent fragmentation and redundancy. But at the same time, the users must have the data they need to perform their duties.

Data administration must balance the central control of data with the users' need for data. If the balance swings to user control, there will be fragmentation, redundancy, and lower productivity. If the balance swings to absolute control, user needs will not be met and productivity will decline.

Data administration must promote the free flow of data to users based on their needs, yet control the design, security, and integrity of that data. Standard policies and procedures will help to achieve these objectives. The best approach to developing standards is to have users involved in their preparation.

Data administration includes acquisition, installation, and maintenance of the database management system and the information resource directory. These activities include selecting the database management system and the directory most suitable to the company's environment.

Above all, data administration must be involved in planning. The information plans must be an integral part of the company's plans. Data administration must be involved in the company's strategic planning and must develop tactical plans for data management that support the company plans.

Traditionally, systems people could not produce systems fast enough. Today, end users have hardware and software available to them but cannot get to the data they need. Data administration must resolve this conflict.

One way to resolve the conflict is to realize that there cannot be absolute control and peak productivity. There must be a compromise between reasonable control and reasonable productivity. This compromise must be oriented toward achieving company goals.

This compromise can be achieved by identifying major backbone systems, support applications, and ad hoc capability. Backbone systems are the major systems developed and maintained by the professional systems development staff. Support applications are smaller systems that can be developed and maintained by either the professional staff or by the users. Ad hoc capability supports the minor, transient requests from users.

Data administration is an important function that is the key to a successful database environment. That function must be established and given the authority to manage the data resource. That management requires both professional skills and the ability to pull people together for a common goal.

User Involvement

Direct user involvement has been emphasized several times. Users must be involved in the design of applications and databases. Users must be involved in developing and enforcing standards. Above all, users must be involved in planning.

It is the users' right to be involved in the development of systems. But along with that right comes a responsibility. Too often, users demand the rights but ignore the responsibilities.

Users have the responsibility for correct specification of data. They have the knowledge and experience about what data is needed and how it is used. That knowledge and experience, combined with the technical skills of professional data processors, produces a synergy that maximizes development productivity.

Users have the responsibility for cost-effective use of data and databases. With the availability of hardware and software, such as personal computers, information centers, and ad hoc capability, users have a tremendous opportunity to obtain the data they need. However, the indiscriminate use of those resources can cripple any company.

Users have the responsibility for designating levels of security and designating who has access authority. They must also determine policies for dissemination of data and disclosure of confidential information. Data administration may control the access, but it is the user that designates that access.

Users have the responsibility for the design, development, and operation of their own systems for the life of the system. With the information explosion and the increase in computer literacy there is a tendency for users to develop "quick and dirty" applications that are the key to operation of the business, then lose interest and turn those applications over to the professional staff to operate and maintain. This only adds to the maintenance effort and delays development of major information systems.

If users are to design and maintain their own systems, they have the responsibility to learn and use the proper design methods and techniques. It is the professionals' responsibility to define methods that are easy to understand and use and to train users in those methods. The users must be committed to using those methods.

Users also have the responsibility to contribute to development, and enforcement, of standard policies and procedures. Standards must be established for the design, development, and use of applications and databases, and users must be involved in that effort.

There cannot be a double standard where professionals follow one set of standards and users follow another. This only leads to fragmentation, not to integration, and results in lower productivity and missed goals. There must be one set of standards covering the range of applications from backbone systems to ad hoc capability, and all developers must follow those standards.

Companies can survive the dynamic business environment and the information explosion only if users are directly involved in the development and use of applications and databases. Users need to be involved, they have the right to be involved, and they have a responsibility when involved. When this involvement is optimized, the company will succeed.

Information Resource Directory

A successful database environment must be supported by some type of information resource directory. Many unsuccessful database environments have failed because they were not supported by a good information resource directory. If a company wants a successful database environment, it must implement, and maintain, a good information resource directory.

A good information resource directory contains data about the company's data: the meta-data. It can be anything from an index card file to a fully automated system with its own database, query language, and report generator. Generally, the more powerful the information resource directory, the more support it provides. However, any directory is better than nothing.

A good information resource directory has a dictionary capability and a directory capability. The dictionary portion provides a definition of each member entered. Members may be data attributes, programs, procedures, physical files, job streams, reports, documents, etc.

The directory portion provides a reference to the relations between members. These relations include which members use and which members constitute other members. It is a very powerful feature to be able to determine relationships between members and the use of each member.

An information resource directory is generally not good for text processing, graphics, or storage of source code. These needs can best be met by other hardware and software. However, the information resource directory can be used as a directory to where these documents are kept.

The purpose of an information resource directory is to increase productivity. This is accomplished by providing a central repository for meta-data that anyone can access. However, to be useful and provide the maximum benefit, it must be kept current.

A current, complete, accurate information resource directory is mandatory for good application and database development. After-the-fact documentation with an information resource directory is no better than traditional after-the-fact documentation. In fact, it may be worse because the perception is that an automated information resource directory is current. If the data is not current, but is accepted as current, wrong decisions can be made and productivity can be severely affected.

However, an information resource directory can be overused. For example, during initial design many alternatives are evaluated and many design changes are made. While the design is dynamic, data should not be put in an information resource directory. But as soon as the design is stable, the data should be documented in the information resource directory.

An information resource directory can be used for retrofit documentation of an existing system. Although this documentation may be useful, it is usually not as extensive as the documentation of a new system. Generally, a retrofit includes only the definitions necessary to maintain the existing system, interface to a new system, or develop a new system.

The structure of the members in an information resource directory is important. If the members are not well-structured and the relations are not well defined, the full advantages of an information resource directory will never be utilized.

The important thing to remember when developing the structure of an information resource directory is not to confuse the organization of the people, the organization of the applications, and the organization of the data. If these three organizations are kept separate at the higher level, the remainder of the members usually fall into place.

Once the structure of the information resource directory is determined, the parameters for each member type can be defined. These parameters depend on the needs of each individual company. As the information resource directory is used, the parameters may need to be adjusted to be useful.

An information resource directory is an extremely powerful tool for developing and documenting applications and databases. The correct selection, implementation, and use of an information resource directory will improve the productivity and quality of development. This improvement results in successful systems and a successful company.

SUMMARY

Knowledge is one key to the success of a business. Those companies that have the knowledge they need when and where they need it can compete in the dynamic business environment. When they compete successfully, they can survive.

Having the knowledge requires managing data to produce information that is retained as knowledge. Managing data successfully includes managing both the people resource and the information resource. Both resources must be managed successfully to have the knowledge to survive.

The technology of information management is changing at a rapid rate. Good management requires an awareness of industry trends and of current technology. It also requires skill at deciding what technology will best support the needs of the company.

Many companies are following better business practices which require better information practices. Part of these better practices is direct involvement of users in planning, developing, and using information systems. Including the user creates a synergy that will meet company goals in the most optimum manner.

To meet company goals, many companies are following a business-driven information management strategy. The needs of the business are driving the development of information systems. As a result, information planning is an integral part of business planning.

Good planning and good information management will produce information to meet the company needs and will increase the productivity of people. When people work together with good techniques under good management, goals are met. When goals are met, the company succeeds and everyone gains.

STUDY QUESTIONS

1. What is knowledge?
2. What is information resource management?

   3. Why is management commitment important?
   4. Why is planning important to a successful database environment?
   5. What are the functions of data administration?
   6. What are the users' responsibilities?
   7. What is an information resource directory?
   8. Why is an information resource directory necessary?
   9. Why is productivity important?
  10. What can increase a company's chance for success?

8

CONCLUSION

Traditional data processing was characterized by applications that supported the core function of a business. These applications were largely record driven or transaction driven. Master files were processed sequentially and usually resided on cards or magnetic tape.

Computer hardware was relatively slow and expensive and application design was oriented to minimum processing cost. People were relatively inexpensive and could spend time optimizing applications for the hardware. These "data-processing wizards" were the people that designed, built, and often operated each application.

The data files were oriented to the applications they supported. They were structured for, and contained data needed by, a specific application. This led to high data redundancy between applications and resulted in storage anomalies and inaccurate data.

Companies used their applications more for history or after-the-fact review than for managing or planning. The business environment was relatively static and after-the-fact review was acceptable. There was little need for current "real-time" data.

However, nothing remains the same for very long. The business environment became more dynamic and more current data was needed to support the company. Applications became information systems and became oriented to direct support of all aspects of the company.

Computer hardware costs continue to decrease and their capability continues to increase. Personnel costs, however, continue to increase, causing a shift in emphasis from hardware optimization to people optimization. One way to optimize people is to let users be involved in the design of their systems.

The concepts of data storage began to change with the shift from hardware to people optimization. Data sharing was encouraged between applications and between users, and data was beginning to be stored independent of the applications it supported. Databases were designed containing multiple data files and began to be structured by subject rather than by application need.

Data management evolved as a discipline to manage databases. As systems massaged larger amounts of data and produced information, the concepts of information management evolved. Today, data and information are accepted as a resource and are managed like other resources in the company.

The design of data files was based largely on application needs and computer hardware optimization. Application design was also largely oriented to computer hardware. Very little, if any, effort was spent on data design.

As databases and database management systems emerged, more emphasis was placed on data design. Strategic data planning is becoming part of company strategic planning, and data modeling is becoming an accepted practice. Logical data design, followed by physical file implementation and user involvement in the design process, are becoming common.

Just as things have not remained static in the past, they will not remain static in the future. There will continue to be changes in the business environment, in company and user needs, and in technology. Some of these changes are predictable and can be incorporated in planning.

The business environment will become even more dynamic and will require better, more current information. Information planning will become an integral part of business planning. Knowledge will become as important in the future as information is today.

On-line systems and communication networks will be the standard and not the exception. Distributed processing and distributed databases will become commonplace. Users will become involved in building and operating their own systems.

Hardware will continue to improve with database machines, parallel processors, and content-addressable memory. Personal computers, workstations, and information centers will be as common as telephones, typewriters, and copy machines are today. Traditional hardware will be smaller in size, larger in capacity, and faster.

Business systems will evolve to decision support systems, knowledge-based systems, and expert systems. Graphics capability will be as common as text is today. Source languages will improve both to handle the new systems and to improve the productivity of· people developing and using those new systems.

Databases will become data oriented rather than file oriented. Systems will become more data oriented rather than strictly process oriented. Database access will range from predefined production access to ad hoc capability.

In short, these trends mean a bigger, better, faster, and more complex environment. This environment demands better management. Information resource management is the discipline emerging to provide that better management.

Along with information resource management comes information engineering. It is a precise engineering discipline for designing and developing information, and is a peer to software engineering and hardware engineering. Information engineering is the forerunner of knowledge engineering.

Any system of the future will consist of hardware, software, and information. All three must be integrated for a successful system. All three are subject to the principles of planning, modeling, and engineering.

Any successful system must also be well-designed. A good design is based on a good design method. A good design method must meet several requirements.

It must be based on sound theory, yet it must be practical and easy to use. It must consistently produce the same result regardless of who uses the method. It must also be reproducible so as to produce the same result with the same input.

A good design method must improve productivity. It must be subject to automation where possible, and allow designers to put their efforts into alternatives, thought, and decisions. It must put the emphasis on design rather than on construction and testing.

It must be both effective and efficient, and produce a high-quality product. It must produce databases that are stable over time, yet allow for flexible software and hardware. It must be oriented to meeting company needs.

The data-structured database design method is based on set theory, relational theory, and normalization theory. It will consistently produce the same result with the same input regardless of the designer.

Major portions of the design method can be automated, which improves the productivity of people using the method. It places emphasis on logical design before physical implementation, and it emphasizes complete design before implementation. It is also compatible with, and an integral part of, data-structured system development.

Data-structured database design is driven by company needs in a dynamic business environment. It allows top-down strategic planning and bottom-up analysis of details. It is oriented both to "doing the right thing" and to "doing it right."

It allows the data to be structured by subject and the application to be structured by business activity. It produces databases that are extremely stable structurally and are minimally affected by changes in application structure. It also provides the flexibility necessary to meet changing business needs.

The data-structured database design method itself is dynamic and can change with changing trends. It meets the needs of today's systems and database requirements. However, the method can be enhanced to meet the needs of semistructured and unstructured databases and knowledge bases when they arrive.

As the environment becomes more complex, the tools to survive in that environment must become more sophisticated, and our skills at using those tools must become equally sophisticated. If we are to survive tomorrow's environment, we must learn how to manage today's environment. If we cannot manage today's environment, we surely cannot survive tomorrow's.

POSTSCRIPT

Interpersonal communications is the ultimate key to productivity improvement. Too often we concentrate on systems, procedures, methods, and standards, yet ignore the people issues. But the best systems, the best procedures, the best methods, and the best standards will fail without people.

Good system development must go hand in hand with good people management. The personal side of information systems is as important as the technical side, perhaps even more important. People issues can make, or break, a system regardless of the quality or features of that system.

We are leaving an age where people exploited the computer and are entering an age where the computer will exploit the human mind. We are entering an age of knowledge ware, mind ware, artificial intelligence, and robotics. We are beginning to emulate people.

But with all this sophistication we can still cripple progress with unresolved people issues. People need to be brought together and work together to solve both people and technical issues. When people work together, there is a synergy that produces a product far larger than the sum of the parts.

As people work together we need to watch them and recognize individual actions and reactions. We need to be aware of the principles and techniques of interpersonal communications, and to use them to promote personal involvement and personal growth. Only through the involvement and growth of people can we ever hope to achieve the ultimate productivity.

APPENDIX:

VIDEO RENTAL CASE STUDY

The data-structured design method is equally applicable to both large and small systems. The example shown in Chapter 6 may have been too large and detailed for a small company designing a small system. The example described here is more beneficial to those wanting to design smaller systems.

The situation is a small video rental store, typical of those seen in many cities and towns. This video rental store is having difficulty servicing customers during peak periods. The owner has already determined that he cannot afford to hire additional help; however, he can obtain a personal computer.

The owner's question is whether or not a personal computer can help him with his peak-period problems. To determine if it can help, a simple system design can be performed, including a database design. Once the system is designed, the owner can determine if the personal computer can help with the peak periods.

PROBLEM STATEMENT

The apparent problem is a long line of customers waiting to rent videotapes they have selected. These customers have already selected the videotapes by reviewing those available on shelves and taking the empty carton to the rental counter. There is no question of the videotape being available; the carton on the shelf indicates that the videotape is available for rental.

By analyzing the apparent problem, it was found that the delay was due to the length of time required to fill out a rental contract form, list all the videotapes being rented on that form, and verify the customer information. Therefore, the first problem was stated as follows:

Long delays in renting videotapes due to the length of time required to complete and verify the rental contract form.

During the problem analysis a second problem was also identified. Many of the customers wanted to know if the rental store had obtained copies of certain videotapes. The owner had, on occasion, attempted to develop an index of videotapes available, but due to the frequency of arrival of new videotapes and the length of time to type the index, an index to videotapes had never been produced. Therefore, the second problem was stated as follows:

The delay in renting videotapes is further delayed by frequent questions about the availability of videotapes.

These two problems are the cause of the long delays in renting videotapes. When these problems are resolved, the problem of long delays will be resolved. Any other problems are outside the scope of this particular project.

NEEDS STATEMENT

Once the problems have been determined, the needs can be stated. The needs must be within the scope of the problems and must answer the problems completely. These needs, when met, will resolve the problems.

The first problem can be resolved by developing a method to print automatically on the rental contract the customer information and the titles of the videotapes being rented. This would allow the customer to sign the rental agreement, pay for the rental, and depart with a minimum of delay. Therefore, the first need was stated as follows:

A method to print a rental contract automatically, including the customer information and the titles of the videotape being rented.

The second problem can be resolved by maintaining a file of videotapes available, printing that file periodically, and making a list of titles available to customers. This printed listing could be taken to any quick-print shop for volume printing, which would allow customers to take a list of available titles with them. Therefore, the second need was stated as follows:

Maintain a list of available videotape titles for customers to take with them for review.

These two needs will answer the problems as defined, and, when met, will resolve the problems as defined. Neither of these needs is outside the scope of the problems, and the needs fully answer the problems.

BUSINESS ENVIRONMENT

Once the scope of the problem is known, a business entity model can be developed. This business entity model must be within the scope of the project and must fully define the scope of the project. The business entity model for this project is shown in Figure A.1.

There are only three business entities in this model: the video rental company, the vendor who supplies new videotapes, and the customer renting videotapes. Any other business entities, such as an accounting firm, the bank, or janitorial services, are outside the scope of the project and are not shown on the business entity model.

The business transactions are described briefly below. These are the only business transactions that are within the scope of the project.

> *New Video Titles:* the arrival of new videotape cassettes from the video vendor
>
> *Video Tape Index:* the list of videotapes available from the video rental store
>
> *Customer Data:* the data about each customer that appears on the video rental contract
>
> *Video Rental Request:* the request for videotapes from the customer in the form of one or more cartons from the shelf
>
> *Video Rental Contract:* the signed rental contract showing customer information and the videotapes being rented

BUSINESS INFORMATION MODEL

Once the business transactions are known, the system can be designed. The business information model shows the architecture of the system that will meet the needs. This model will contain all the transactions from the business entity model.

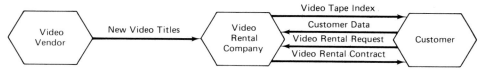

Figure A.1   Business entity model for videotape rental.

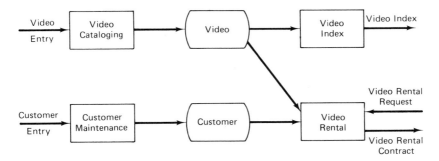

Figure A.2   Business information model for videotape rental.

The business information model for this system is shown in Figure A.2. The model contains four processes, two data storages, and ten data flows.

New videocassettes are received and cataloged in the Video Cataloging process. A unique Video Number is placed on the videotape cassette, the videotape information is entered into the Video Title storage, and the videotape cassettes are stored. The empty videotape carton is placed on the shelf for customers to review.

New customers are registered with the video rental company in the Customer Maintenance process by obtaining specific customer data, storing it in the Customer storage, and issuing the customer a card to be used for renting videotapes. This card contains the customer information and a unique Customer Number.

After new titles are received and cataloged, a list of titles is printed by the Video Index process and sent to a quick-print shop. The printed Video Index is then available for customer use.

The videotape cassettes are rented to the Customer in the Video Rental process. When a customer comes to the counter with a request for one or more videotapes, the videotape cassettes are obtained from storage, and a rental contract is printed showing the customer information and the videotapes being rented. After payment the customer leaves with the videotape cassettes and a copy of the rental contract.

The five external data flows represent the five business transactions on the business entity model. The other five data flows are internal data flows between storages and processes. The two data storages contain Video data and Customer data.

This business information model shows the total architecture for the video rental system as defined in the problems and needs statements. Any additional processes, data flows, or data storages would be outside the scope of the project.

DATA DEFINITION

When the business information model is completed, the data is defined for each data flow on the business information model. The output data flows are defined first so that an output data entity model may be developed.

The output data flows are the Video Index and the Video Rental Contract. The output data structure for the Video Index is shown in Figure A.3 and the required data structure is shown in Figure A.4. The calculated attributes in the output data structure are replaced with the supportive attribute in the required data structure.

The output data structure for the Video Rental Contract is shown in Figure A.5. The required data structure is shown in Figure A.6. The Video Rental Contract in the output data structure has been dropped since it contains no data. Customer has been added in the required data structure since customer is the subject entity.

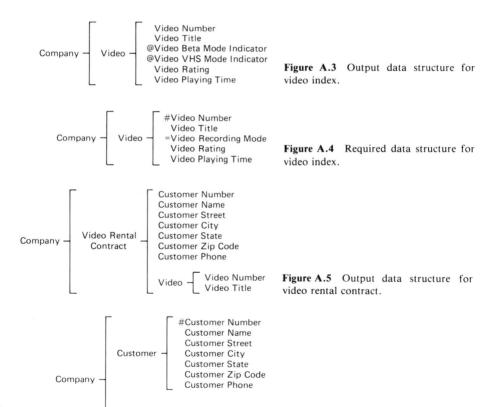

Figure A.3 Output data structure for video index.

Figure A.4 Required data structure for video index.

Figure A.5 Output data structure for video rental contract.

Figure A.6 Required data structure for video rental contract.

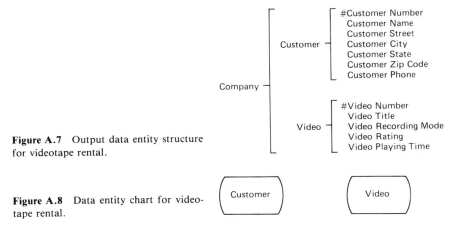

Figure A.7   Output data entity structure for videotape rental.

Figure A.8   Data entity chart for video-tape rental.

The output data entity structure for these two outputs is shown in Figure A.7. Two subject data storages are needed to supply data to the output processes. The Video storage contains data about each video in the store and the Customer storage contains data about each customer renting videos from the store.

The data entity chart is shown in Figure A.8. There is only one access path to each storage. Customer Number is the primary key and the only access path to customer data, and Video Number is the primary key and the only access path to Video Titles.

The inputs to the system are the Video Title Entry, Customer Data, and Video Rental Request. The data entered on the inputs must maintain all the data in the data storages, but must not add data that is not needed from the data storages.

The input data structure for the Video Entry is shown in Figure A.9, and the necessary data structure is shown in Figure A.10. The two data structures are identical except for the primary key identified in the necessary data structure.

The input data structure for Customer Entry is shown in Figure A.11, and the necessary data structure is shown in Figure A.12. Again, the two data

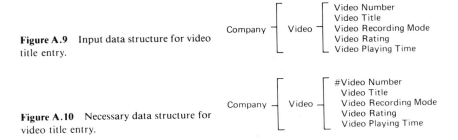

Figure A.9   Input data structure for video title entry.

Figure A.10   Necessary data structure for video title entry.

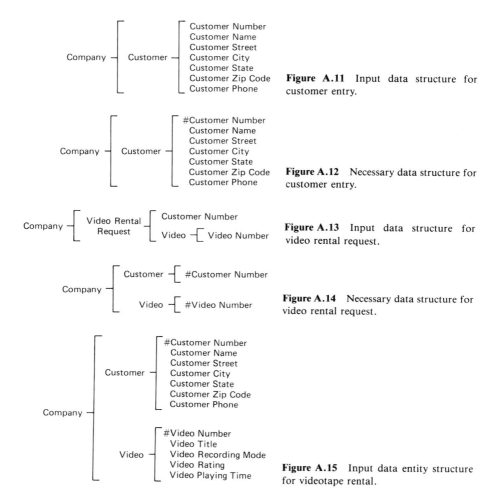

Figure A.11 Input data structure for customer entry.

Figure A.12 Necessary data structure for customer entry.

Figure A.13 Input data structure for video rental request.

Figure A.14 Necessary data structure for video rental request.

Figure A.15 Input data entity structure for videotape rental.

structures are identical except for the primary key indicator on the necessary data structure.

The input data structure for the Vendor Rental Request is shown in Figure A.13, and the necessary data structure is shown in Figure A.14. Each rental request contains one customer and one or more video numbers. The necessary data structure shows primary keys for the Customer Number and Video Number.

The input data entity structure is shown in Figure A.15, and the data entity chart is shown in Figure A.16. The structure and chart are both identical to the output structure and chart shown in Figures A.7 and A.8.

Figure A.16   Input data entity chart for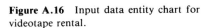
videotape rental.

LOGICAL DATABASE

When the output data entity model is completed, it is compared with the business information model to verify that the architecture, specifically the data storages, match the data entity model. In this example there is a match. However, as systems become larger, there may not be a match and adjustments will need to be made.

When the input data entity model is completed, it is also compared to the business information model. In this small system there is agreement and no adjustments are needed.

The input data entity model and output data entity model are then compared. If there is an inconsistency in either entities or attributes, these inconsistencies must be resolved. In this example the entities and attributes agree.

When the input and output data entity models agree, the complete data entity model is prepared by merging the two models. In this example the models are identical, including the access paths, so the total data entity model would be exactly the same as either the input or the output model.

PHYSICAL DATABASE

Once the logical database has been defined, the physical database can be built. Each data entity will become a physical file unless there are special criteria for nesting, splitting, or eliminating data entities. In this example each data entity will become a separate physical file.

During data definition each attribute was fully defined, usually to a data dictionary. Once the physical files are determined, the attribute definitions are used to build physical records. If the physical records were very long, the frequency of use of each attribute would be used to place it in the physical record. However, in this small example the frequency of use is of minor importance.

Each access path will become a key or super-key in the physical file. In this example there is only one access path to each file and only one key to each path. The structure of the physical file is shown in Figure A.17.

The physical file will be generated according to this structure. Any DBMS, or other access method, can be used. Physical optimization may be made after a period of operation; however, in this small system there will probably not be any physical optimization.

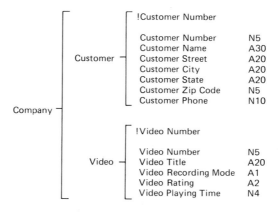

Figure A.17   Physical file structure for videotape rental.

SUMMARY

Process logic will be developed for each process on the business information model. This process logic will be used to develop the source code for the programs. The logical views of data are defined on the data structures for the data flows into and out of each process.

The system as designed does meet the needs as defined. After a review of this design the video rental store owner determined that the system was feasible and would meet his needs. Based on that decision the system will be built.

This system forms a base that can be enhanced if desired. Each enhancement would go through the same steps described above and would solve one or more problems encountered by the video rental store. These enhancements are typical of the normal business environment today.

GLOSSARY

Access Path   A navigational route between entities in a database.

Aggregation   *See* Attribute Aggregation.

Ampersand (&)   Attribute identifier on an output data structure indicating a parameter.

Antonym   Words with opposite meanings (i.e., "sad" and "happy").

Asterisk (*)   Attribute identifier on a required or necessary data structure indicating a primary, compound, or composite key not used for access.

At Sign (@)   Attribute identifier on an output data structure indicating a calculated attribute.

Attribute   A logical data element with definition but no physical parameters.

Attribute Aggregation   Adding attributes from decoupled entities into master subject entities.

Attribute Identifier   A symbol preceding an attribute name to identify a special use of that attribute.

Binding   Establishes a physical access path to data.

Business Activity   A task, or set of tasks, to process a business event.

Business Entity   An entity representing a business unit composed of people.

Business Entity Model   Architecture of the business world from a company's perspective.

Business Event   An arrival of an input or a demand for an output.

Business Information Model   Highest-level architecture of processes, data flows, and storages for the business.

Business Transaction   A set of data moving between business entities.

Child Entity   *See* Subordinate Entity.

Cohesion   The degree of data flow within modules.

Colon (:)   Attribute identifier on a necessary data structure indicating a derived attribute.

Column   A vertical column of data in a relational table; *same as* Attribute.

Composite Key   Two or more attributes from two or more entities used to identify uniquely each occurrence in an entity.

Composition   *See* Data Structure Composition.

Compound Foreign Key   A foreign key composed of two or more attributes from a parent entity.

Compound Key   Two or more attributes from the same entity used to identify uniquely each occurrence in that entity.

Concatenated Keys   A key consisting of two or more attributes.

Conceptual Schema   A logical data structure that resolves problems with the two-schema approach.

Coupling   The degree of data flow between modules.

Dashed Line   A data relation on the data entity model or an access path on the database model.

Data   Individual pieces of information.

Data Attribute   *See* Attribute.

Database   A collection of data designed to be used by a variety of users.

Database Environment   The building of a logical and physical subject database structured independently of the application and based on a formal design method.

Database Management   The method of managing a database environment.

Database Management System   Computer-based system to define, create, and maintain automated data.

Database Model   A model showing the architecture of the physical database.

Data Element   Basic unit of information that cannot be further subdivided.

Data Entity   An entity representing a group of attributes describing a data subject or a transaction.

Data Entity Model   A model showing the architecture of the logical database.

Data File   A physical file of data.

Data Flow   The movement of data to and from storages and processes in a system.

Data Flowchart   A chart or diagram showing data storages, logic processes, and data flows.

Data Group   A subset of data with the same characteristics.

Data Independence   The structure of data storage is independent of the structure of process logic.

Data Integrity   In the relational model, integrity assures that each occurrence in an entity is unique.

Data Item   A physical data element with definition and physical parameters.

Data Management   The method of managing data.

Data Model   An association between data items.

Data Redundancy   *See* Redundant Data.

Data Relation   A logical relationship between two data entities; *see* One-to-Many Relation; Many-to-One Relation; Many-to-Many Relation.

Data Security   Assuring that data is safe from unauthorized access, alteration, and destruction.

Data Set   A collection of data attributes in a data structure.

Data Sharing   The sharing of subject data by many applications.

Data Storage   A logical file of data.

Data Structure   A hierarchy of entities and their attributes.

Data Structure Composition   Building a data structure using a hierarchy of entities and their attributes.

Data Structure Decomposition   Decoupling the data entities in a required or necessary data structure and aggregating the attributes by entity.

Data Transaction   A set of data moving between data processes.

Decimal Point (.)   Prefixes an attribute name on a data structure, indicating that the entity name is missing.

Decision Support System   An automated system that provides information to support the decision-making process.

Decomposition   *See* Data Structure Decomposition.

Decouple   Separate entities in a data structure.

Deletion Anomaly   The loss of parent data stored in a subordinate entity when the last subordinate occurrence is deleted.

Dollar Sign ($)   Attribute identifier indicating an attribute added to the physical database.

Domain   *See* Column.

Entity   A person, place, thing, or event; *see* Data Entity; Business Entity.

Entity Separation   Decoupling entities in a required or necessary data structure.

Equal Sign (=)   Attribute identifier on a required data structure indicating a supportive attribute.

Event   *See* Business Event.

Exclamation Mark (!)   Attribute identifier on the physical data structure indicating a super-key.

Expert System   An automated system that performs tasks equal to human experts.

External Schema   A logical data structure.

First Normal Form   Isolation of repeating groups in a data structure.

Foreign Key   Primary key of the parent entity stored in the subordinate entity used to access the parent occurrence.

Functional Decomposition   Decomposing a business to develop a business information model.

Hierarchical Database   A tree structure where each record is subordinate to only one parent record.

Homonym   Words with the same pronunciation and different meanings (i.e., sale and sail).

Information   Assimilated and condensed data.

Information Resource Management   A formal discipline for managing data to produce information that is retained as knowledge.

Input Data Entity Model   A data entity model based solely on necessary data structures.

Input Data Structure   A data structure representing data on an input document.

Input Logical Database   The logical database developed solely from necessary data structures.

Input-Only Process   A logic process with only inputs and no outputs.

Insertion Anomaly   The loss of parent data stored in a subordinate entity when there are no subordinate occurrences.

Interface   Boundary between a new system and an existing system.

Internal Data Flow   Data flow between processes and storages, not into or out of the system.

Internal Schema   A physical data structure.

Inverted Data Relation   Defining an attribute as an entity and assigning other attributes to characterize the new entity.

Inverted List   List of keys for an inverted data relation.

Iterative   Repetitive.

Key   An attribute used to navigate between entities in the database.

Key Group   A set of one or more attributes representing a unique access to an entity.

Knowledge   Retained information.

Knowledge-Based System   A system to maintain and access a scientific or technical body of knowledge.

Left Caret (<)   Attribute identifier on an input data structure indicating data on an input document not entered into a system.

Logical Data Accesses   The key groups needed for accessing entities in the data entity model.

Logical Database   The entities, attributes, data relations, logical accesses, and keys defining the logical data processed in a system.

Logical Data Relations   The relationship between data entities in the data entity model.

Logical Data Structure   The structure of entities and attributes in the data entity model.

Logical Record   *See* Occurrence.

Logical View   A set of data from the total database that is needed by a unit of process logic.

Many-to-Many Relation   An occurrence in one entity is related to many occurrences in another entity, and vice versa.

Many-to-One Relation   A data relation of many subordinate entities to one parent entity.

Meta-Data   Data defining the data used in an information system.

Meta-Model   Graphic representation, terminology, and rules describing logical database design.

Minus Sign ($-$)   Attribute identifier on a required or necessary data structure, indicating a secondary key.

Model   Preliminary representation of the arrangement and relationship of elements in a system.

Necessary Data Structure   A data structure showing attributes used to maintain the data base.

Net Data Flow   Data flows into and out of the system.

Normalization   The grouping of like attributes in their least divisible form.

Normalization Theory   Defines how entities are formed to capture their inherent nature, structure, and meaning.

Occurrence   A unique logical record in an entity.

One-to-Many Relation   A data relation of one parent entity with many subordinate entities.

One-to-One Relation   An occurrence in one entity is related to only one occurrence in another entity, and vice versa.

Output Data Entity Model   A data entity model based solely on required data structures.

Output Data Structure   A data structure representing data on an output report.

Output Logical Database   The logical database developed solely from required data structures.

Output-Only Process   A logic process with only outputs and no inputs.

Ownership Controversy   Disagreement over who owns the data in a company-wide database environment.

Parent Entity   An entity that contains one or more child, or subordinate, entities.

Physical Database   The files, data items, physical access paths, and keys defining the physical storage of data.

Physical File   *See* Data File.

Plus Sign (+)   Attribute identifier on a required or necessary data structure, indicating a foreign key.

Pound Sign (#)   Attribute identifier on a required or necessary data structure, indicating a primary key.

Primary Key   A single attribute used to uniquely identify each occurrence in an entity.

Process Logic   The logic processes defining the actions taken on data in a process.

Prototype   The first of its kind that is repeatedly enhanced to meet an end objective.

Question Mark (?)   Attribute identifier indicating an attribute in question.

Quote Mark (')   Attribute identifier on an output data structure indicating a literal.

Redundant Data   Data that is stored in more than one entity.

Read-Only Storage   A data storage that is used but never updated.

Relation   A two-dimensional table with rows and columns.

Relational Database   A database architecture with no predefined subordinate relations.

Relational Model   The mathematical model defining a relational database.

Relational Theory   The mathematical principles supporting the relational model.

Relationship   A data relation between two entities.

Repetitive   Occurs or performed again and again until some condition is met.

Required Data Structure   A data structure showing attributes needed from the database.

Retrofit   Adjusting an existing system to meet new design standards without any enhancements to the system.

Right Caret (>)   Attribute identifier on an input data structure indicating data entered into the system but not stored on the database.

Row   A record in a relational table.

Schema   A data structure.

Secondary Key   Attribute that is not a primary key but is used for access to an entity.

Second Normal Form   Removal of partial key dependencies in a data structure.

Separation   *See* Entity Separation.

Set Theory   Mathematical principles for forming and manipulating sets of data.

Solid Line   A data flow on a business information model or data flowchart, or a business transaction on a business entity model.

Storage Anomaly   Collectively includes deletion, insertion, and update anomalies.

Subentity   An entity that is subordinate to another entity in a data structure.

Subject Database   A database environment where data is stored by subject.

Subject Entity   An entity representing a single subject of data, i.e., customer.

Subordinate Entity   An entity that is subordinate to, or a child of, a higher-level parent entity.

Super-Key   A physical key composed of two or more data items.

Synonym   Two different words with the same meaning.

Third Normal Form   Removal of interattribute dependencies in a data structure.

Time-Relational Model   A relational model with comprehensive time-processing capabilities.

Total Logical Database   Logical database derived from combining the input and output data entity models.

Transaction   A set of data that is moving between two points; *see* Business Transaction; Data Transaction.

Transaction Entity   An entity representing a data transaction moving between processes.

Tuple   *See* Occurrence.

Update Anomaly   The situation where all occurrences of redundant data are not consistently updated.

User View   *See* Logical View.

Value   Contents of an attribute.

Write-Only Storage   A data storage that is updated but never used.

BIBLIOGRAPHY

BRACKETT, M. H., *Developing Data Structured Information Systems*. Topeka, Kansas: Ken Orr & Associates, Inc., 1983.

CODD, E. F., A Relational Model of Data for Large Shared Data Banks, *Commun. ACM*, Vol. 13, No. 6, June 1970.

DATE, C. J., *An Introduction to Data Base Systems*, Vols. I and II. Reading, Mass.: Addison-Wesley, 1982.

DEMARCO, T., *Structured Analysis and Systems Specification*. New York: Yourdon Press, 1978.

FLAVIN, M., *Fundamental Concepts of Information Modeling*. New York: Yourdon Press, 1981.

GANE, C. P., and SARSON, T., *Structured Systems Analysis: Tools and Techniques*. New York: Improved System Technologies, Inc., 1977.

JACKSON, M. A., *Principles of Program Design*. New York: Academic Press, 1975.

JACKSON, M. A., *System Development*. Englewood Cliffs, N.J.: Prentice-Hall, 1983.

MARTIN, J., *Principles of Data Base Management*. Englewood Cliffs, N.J.: Prentice-Hall, 1976.

MARTIN, J., *Computer Data Base Organization*, 2nd ed. Englewood Cliffs, N.J.: Prentice-Hall, 1977.

MARTIN, J., *Strategic Data Planning Methodologies*. Englewood Cliffs, N.J.: Prentice-Hall, 1982.

NOLAN, R. L., Managing the Crises in Data Processing, *Harvard Business Review*, March–April 1979.

ORR, K. T., *Structured Systems Development*. New York: Yourdon Press, 1977.

ORR, K. T., *Structured Requirements Definition*. Topeka, Kansas: Ken Orr & Associates, Inc., 1981.

PETERS, L. J., *Software Design: Methods and Techniques*. New York: Yourdon Press, 1981.

WARNIER, J. D., *Logical Construction of Systems*. New York: Van Nostrand Reinhold, 1979.

WEINBERG, V., *Structured Analysis*. New York: Yourdon Press, 1978.

YOURDON, E., *Techniques of Program Structure and Design*. Englewood Cliffs, N.J.: Prentice-Hall, 1975.

YOURDON, E., and CONSTANTINE, L. L., *Structured Design*. Englewood Cliffs, N.J.: Prentice-Hall, 1979.

INDEX